Benjamin West
AMERICAN PAINTER
AT THE ENGLISH COURT

Benjamin West
AMERICAN PAINTER
AT THE ENGLISH COURT

June 4–August 20, 1989

The Baltimore Museum of Art

LIBRARY OF CONGRESS CATALOGING-IN-PUBLICATION DATA

West, Benjamin, 1738–1820.
    Benjamin West, American painter at the English Court: June
  4–August 20, 1989.
      p.   cm.
    Catalog of an exhibition held at the Baltimore Museum of Art.
    Essay by Allen Staley.
    Includes bibliographies.
    ISBN 0-912298-64-2
    1. West, Benjamin, 1738–1820—Exhibitions.   2. West Benjamin,
  1738–1820—Criticism and interpretation.   I. Staley, Allen.
  II. Baltimore Museum of Art.   III. Title.   IV. Title: American
  painter at the English court.
  ND237.W45A4   1989
  759.13—dc19   88-36584
                                               CIP

West with his own great soul the canvass warms,
Creates, inspires, impassions human forms,
Spurns critic rules, and seizing safe the heart,
Breaks down the former frightful bounds of Art. . . .

Joel Barlow, *The Columbiad*, 1807

Contents

LENDERS TO THE EXHIBITION

ADDISON GALLERY OF AMERICAN ART, PHILLIPS ACADEMY
Andover, Massachusetts

ALLEN MEMORIAL ART MUSEUM, OBERLIN COLLEGE
Oberlin, Ohio

THE BALTIMORE MUSEUM OF ART

BASS MUSEUM OF ART
Miami

MURIEL AND PHILIP BERMAN
Allentown, Pennsylvania

UNIVERSITY ART GALLERY, STATE UNIVERSITY OF NEW
YORK AT BINGHAMTON

BOB JONES UNIVERSITY
Greenville, South Carolina

THE CARNEGIE MUSEUM OF ART
Pittsburgh

COLUMBIA UNIVERSITY
New York

DEERFIELD ACADEMY
Deerfield, Massachusetts

THE DETROIT INSTITUTE OF ARTS

GEORGE E. DOTY
New York

HER MAJESTY QUEEN ELIZABETH II

FRANKLIN AND MARSHALL COLLEGE
Lancaster, Pennsylvania

DESCENDANTS OF THE 8TH VISCOUNT GALWAY
COURTESY NATIONAL ARMY MUSEUM
London

HIRSCHL & ADLER GALLERIES, INC.
New York

KENNEDY GALLERIES, INC.
New York

KIMBELL ART MUSEUM
Fort Worth

DR. AND MRS. HENRY C. LANDON III
North Wilkesboro, North Carolina

THE LIBRARY OF CONGRESS
Washington, D.C.

LOS ANGELES COUNTY MUSEUM OF ART

THOMAS AND MARGARET MCCORMICK
Norton, Massachusetts

MEMORIAL ART GALLERY OF THE UNIVERSITY
OF ROCHESTER

THE METROPOLITAN MUSEUM OF ART
New York

MILWAUKEE ART MUSEUM

MINT MUSEUM
Charlotte, North Carolina

MOUNT HOLYOKE COLLEGE ART MUSEUM
South Hadley, Massachusetts

NATIONAL GALLERY OF ART
Washington, D.C.

NATIONAL GALLERY OF CANADA
Ottawa

THE NELSON-ATKINS MUSEUM OF ART
Kansas City, Missouri

NEW BRITAIN MUSEUM OF AMERICAN ART
Connecticut

NEW ORLEANS MUSEUM OF ART

NEW YORK STATE HISTORICAL ASSOCIATION
Cooperstown

PENNSYLVANIA ACADEMY OF THE FINE ARTS
Philadelphia

PRIVATE COLLECTIONS

JAMES RICAU, COURTESY THE BROOKLYN MUSEUM

THE ROYAL ACADEMY OF ARTS
London

SAN ANTONIO MUSEUM ASSOCIATION

THE FINE ARTS MUSEUMS OF SAN FRANCISCO

H. SHICKMAN GALLERY
New York

SWARTHMORE COLLEGE
Pennsylvania

THE TOLEDO MUSEUM OF ART

UTAH MUSEUM OF FINE ARTS
Salt Lake City

WADSWORTH ATHENEUM
Hartford, Connecticut

HENRY FRANCIS DU PONT WINTERTHUR MUSEUM
Winterthur, Delaware

YALE CENTER FOR BRITISH ART
New Haven, Connecticut

YALE UNIVERSITY ART GALLERY
New Haven, Connecticut

Foreword

Baltimore's Benjamin West exhibition comprises the realization of a personal ambition conceived almost two decades ago. When I was a graduate student in art history at Yale University, I chose West's *Battle of La Hogue* (acquired by Washington's National Gallery only in 1959) as the subject of a lecture in my museum methods course. I was captivated by the authority and grandeur of West's achievement and, even then, it seemed to me to be a serious oversight in our study of earlier American art that West's work was not better known to a larger audience. It is only now, with this 1989 retrospective exhibition, that a comprehensive group of West's major paintings will be available for careful study, deliberate consideration, and general enjoyment—more than fifty years after the last major showing of this great eighteenth-century artist's work.

It is a tribute to the importance and timeliness of this West retrospective exhibition that every one of our loan requests was granted, representing an unprecedented show of support from public and private collectors alike. Each of West's iconic, signature works is included in the exhibition, even those of grand scale and awesome reputation. From Great Britain, Her Majesty Queen Elizabeth II graciously consented to send five splendid paintings by West spanning the most productive years of the artist's long career. From Ottawa, the National Gallery of Canada sent its national treasure, *The Death of General Wolfe*. From Philadelphia, The Pennsylvania Academy of the Fine Arts agreed to part with its much-beloved *Penn's Treaty with the Indians*. Such generosity springs from a genuine dedication both to the subject and to the public interest, and it is with profound gratitude that we acknowledge the warmth and collegial spirit engendered by this exciting project.

As gratifying as we have found the support and enthusiasm of all of our lenders, we have been especially appreciative of the collaboration of our British colleagues and friends. The exhibition was granted the patronage of Sir Antony Acland, Ambassador of the United Kingdom and Northern Ireland to the United States, and Sir Antony has demonstrated his interest in the project from its inception. In London, we met with the warm endorsement of Sir Oliver Millar, then Surveyor of the Queen's Pictures, from our first meeting at which we proposed what seemed even to us to be a very grand loan request indeed. Sir Oliver's enthusiasm for our project was subsequently shared by his successor, Christopher Lloyd, when he assumed the position of Surveyor, and to each of them we owe an enormous debt of gratitude for the support and influence they brought to bear on our behalf. We are equally grateful to Charles Noble, Assistant to the Surveyor of the Queen's Pictures, and to Marcus Bishop, Registrar of the Queen's Pictures, for all that they have done to assure the efficient management of this exceptional loan from the royal collections.

From the moment we committed our Museum to the definitive Benjamin West exhibition, we knew the success of our project rested upon the collaboration of Professor Allen Staley. We therefore invited his participation as author and curatorial consultant at a very early date in our planning. Despite heavy commitments to the Department of Art History and Archaeology at Columbia University, as well as multiple other publication projects, Professor Staley agreed to prepare the text for Baltimore's exhibition catalogue and to consult with our own Museum's staff on the exhibition's scope and precise contents. As the coauthor of the two-volume catalogue raisonné of West's work, published in 1986, there was simply no other scholar whose expertise and sensitivity could match that of Professor Staley in approaching this subject. We are delighted to be able to introduce West's work to an expanded audience with the distinguished support of Allen Staley. Out of deference to Professor Staley's reputation, the text he prepared for Baltimore's catalogue has been published, at his request, without editorial emendation or abbreviation.

We were extremely fortunate in this ambitious endeavor to have the benefit of substantive expertise on our own Museum's staff. Sona Johnston, Associate Curator of Painting and Sculpture and a specialist in eighteenth and nineteenth-century American art, has devoted a significant part of her time over the past three years to this vital project. She has worked closely with Professor Staley on all phases of the exhibition and publication, and has shown an unswerving commitment to the importance of West's work within the larger context of American and British painting of this period. There is no question that her dedication to the concept of a major West exhibition in America was the essential pivot on which we moved forward. Likewise from the beginning, Curatorial Associate Trish Waters has given her organizational skills to the West project and has coordinated with patience and efficiency the countless administrative details of everything from photography to loan letters, from proofreading to insurance coverage. Sona and Trish together also prepared the Chronology for our publication. Faith Holland extended advice and assistance in both editorial and public information arenas, and we are grateful for her sensitivity and forebearance. Audrey Frantz, Director of Publications, provided her customary level of extraordinary efficiency and careful oversight in producing all of the West publications (including the catalogue, a press kit, an invitation, and other educational printed materials). Melanie Harwood, Senior Registrar, managed the daunting assignment of assuring the secure and timely transport of all loaned objects to and from Baltimore; Karen Nielsen, Director of Design & Installation, Joy Peterson, Assistant Director of Membership & Development, and Susan Badder, Director of Education & Community, all offered their always exceptional support in their respective areas of responsibility. Alex and Caroline Castro of Baltimore's Castro/Arts gave generously, as always, of their extraordinary creative insights to design a magnificent catalogue and other printed materials that appropriately reflect the importance of this event.

Like any international loan exhibition of this magnitude, the Benjamin West exhibition and its accompanying publication comprise a financial commitment of substance. It is therefore with a very special pleasure that I am able to acknowledge the extremely generous support of our several sponsors. Once again, our Museum Trustee Jack Moseley has demonstrated a degree of corporate leadership and philanthropy for which he has become known in our community. For the third major BMA exhibition in recent history (preceded by *Mondrian Drawings and Watercolors* in 1981 and *Oskar Schlemmer* in 1986), Jack Moseley has committed his company's resources, through the USF&G Foundation, to support the Benjamin West exhibition with a magnanimous grant which has assured its success. There are no words adequate to express our admiration and profound gratitude for Mr. Moseley's sustained vision and commitment to the cultural life of our city and its citizens.

We are equally grateful to the National Endowment for the Arts, a federal agency, for its ongoing support of museum programs with reference only to the highest standards of conception and production. And we are especially honored to acknowledge the support of The Henry Luce Fund for Scholarship in American Art, which with its substantial grant for the West publication indicated not only its high regard for the merit of our proposal but also its confidence in our Museum and its publication tradition. The Luce Fund additionally supported the West project with a major grant for essential conservation of loaned paintings, thus further assuring the quality and impact of the exhibition. Finally, we are very grateful for the federal indemnification extended to our British and Canadian loans through the Federal Council on the Arts and the Humanities of the National Endowment for the Arts. Alice M. Whelihan, Indemnity Administrator for the NEA's Museum Program, extended her wise counsel, as she has done so often in the past, in guiding us through the application process, for which we are very grateful.

Profound and ambitious as we believe this exhibition and publication to be, we are equally convinced that *Benjamin West: American Painter at the English Court* will prove to be a revelation and a thrilling experience for a significantly expanded general audience as well. Our Education Department has focused significant programming directed toward our community's young people— a generation ready to be awakened to the drama and grandeur of great narrative painting. For the dedication of our staff in realizing such a goal, I am touched and genuinely appreciative. For the commitment and bold vision of our Trustees in supporting our endeavor, it is a special privilege to extend my personal gratitude to Louise P. Hoblitzell, President, whose committed leadership of the Board makes our achievement possible.

ARNOLD L. LEHMAN
DIRECTOR

Chronology

1738	Born October 10, Springfield, Chester County, Pennsylvania. Youngest of ten children of John and Sarah Pearson West.
circa 1747	In Philadelphia. Meets English artist William Williams who lends him books on painting.
early– mid 1750's	Lives with older sister and husband in Philadelphia. Paints over-mantels for house in Strawberry Alley. Paints Chester County neighbor's children, his first known portraits. Receives instruction in painting from Moravian artist John Valentine Haidt.
1755–1756	In Lancaster, Pennsylvania. Paints portraits and, at encouragement of progressive inventor and gunsmith William Henry, his first historical subject, *The Death of Socrates* (cat. 2).
Summer 1756	Moves permanently to Philadelphia following death of mother; becomes protégé of cultural and intellectual leader Reverend William Smith.
1757–1760	Paints portraits in Philadelphia to earn funds to travel and study abroad.
1759	Journeys to New York to paint portraits.
1760	Sails to Leghorn in Tuscany on ship *Betty Sally*. First American artist to travel to Italy. In Rome, meets Anton Raphael Mengs, leading painter in developing neoclassical style.
1760–1763	Travels in Italy with frequent stays in Rome; paints copies after Titian, Correggio, Mengs, and others for American patrons.
1762	In Venice, meets Richard Dalton, librarian to King George III.
1763	In Rome, paints first royal commission for George III, *Cymon and Iphigenia*, which is much admired. Encouraged by Dalton, leaves Italy in May for London via Paris.
1764	Exhibits three paintings at Society of Artists. Dubbed "the American Raphael." Decides to remain in England.
	Marries Elizabeth Shewell of Philadelphia in St.-Martin-in-the-Fields.
1766	Birth of son, Raphael Lamar West.
1768	Charter member of the Royal Academy of Arts.
1769	Paints *The Departure of Regulus from Rome* (cat. 12) for George III, his first work to enter the royal collection.
1770	Paints *The Death of General Wolfe* (cat. 13) which establishes his reputation.
1771–1772	Paints *Penn's Treaty with the Indians* (cat. 15).
1772	Birth of Benjamin West, Jr.
1776	Publication of William Woollett's highly successful engraving after *The Death of General Wolfe* (cat. 61).
1779–1801	Engaged in various extensive decorative programs at Windsor Castle including Royal Chapel and Audience Chamber.
1791	Succeeds Richard Dalton as Surveyor of the King's Pictures.
1792	Becomes second president of the Royal Academy of Arts after death of Sir Joshua Reynolds.
1796	Paints much-admired sketch for *Death on the Pale Horse* (cat. 38).
	Begins work on decorations for Fonthill Abbey, William Beckford's Gothic Revival country house.
1801	Royal patronage ceases.
1802	On his sole visit outside England, admires in Paris neoclassical paintings of David and Guérin.
1811	Receives record amount of 3,000 guineas for *Christ Healing the Sick* (see cat. 69), one of his most popular works.
1814	Elizabeth Shewell West dies. *Christ Rejected* (see cat. 52) viewed by 240,000 during public exhibition.
1816 and 1820	Publication of John Galt's two-volume *Life of Benjamin West*.
1820	Dies March 11, London. Buried in St. Paul's Cathedral.

Cat. 24. Detail, *Self-Portrait.* (ca. 1776)
Oil on canvas. 30¼ x 25⅛ in. (76.9 x 63.8 cm.)
The Baltimore Museum of Art:
Gift of Dr. Morton K. Blaustein,
Barbara B. Hirschhorn, and Elizabeth B. Roswell,
in Memory of Jacob and Hilda K. Blaustein (BMA 1981.73)

1. Portrait of the Artist

Benjamin West was born on October 10, 1738, in the township of Springfield, Pennsylvania, in what was then Chester County and is now Delaware County, some ten miles west of Philadelphia. The house in which he is traditionally said to have been born still stands on the campus of Swarthmore College. His father, John West, had come to Pennsylvania in 1715 or 1716, leaving behind him in England a pregnant wife, who was soon to die in childbirth. The child of that first marriage, Thomas West, Benjamin's half-brother over twenty years his senior, was brought up in England by his maternal grandparents. In America John West remarried in 1720 and had ten further children. Benjamin was the tenth. John West worked at one time as a cooper, and possibly at other trades, but when West was born he was an innkeeper. In 1743, when the future artist was five years old, the family moved to a new inn on the Darby-Springfield road, and in 1744 they moved again to yet another inn in Newtown Square.[1]

Sarah Pearson, who in 1720 became John West's second wife and in 1738 was to give birth to Benjamin, was the daughter of Thomas Pearson of Marple, immediately to the north of Springfield. Sarah Pearson's and John West's parents were all Quakers—Thomas Pearson had come to Pennsylvania with William Penn in 1682—but neither Sarah Pearson nor John West was recorded as a member of the Society of Friends at the time of their marriage or when their children were born. Sarah Pearson had been read out of meeting in 1717, when she was twenty years old, because of fornication; John West had not come to America as a member in good standing, although three years after his second wife's death in 1756 he did join, or rejoin, the Society.[2] Thus Benjamin West was not born a Quaker. In later life he told visitors from Pennsylvania that "I was once a Quaker and have never left the principle."[3] Strictly speaking, that statement does not seem true; nevertheless the Quaker ambience of the rural communities in which the family lived was of no slight significance for his early life. The fact that the West family could not attend meeting together with its good Quaker neighbors must have been as well.

Our prime source of biographical information about West is a two-volume *Life* published in 1816 and 1820 by the Scottish novelist John Galt. The first volume is full of wildly improbable tales, starting with a quasi-miraculous birth replete with prophecies about his future greatness, and numerous details are at odds with facts that can be ascertained from available records. Nevertheless, Galt presented his book as basically a transcription of what West had told him, and claimed that West read and approved it before it was printed.[4] The volume describing West's boyhood also appeared during his lifetime; so, even if we do not believe it all, we must assume that it tells us what the old artist wanted posterity to believe. Galt's stories, such as a much-quoted one about young Benjamin stealing the hair of the family cat Grimalkin to make his first paintbrushes, often seem no more than trivially amusing anecdotes, but together they add up to a consistent picture of predestined genius triumphing over all odds. Running through many of them as well is the presence of West's mother. When he makes his first drawing, she instantly admires it and encourages him. When he plays hooky from school to stay home and paint, Mrs. West, instead of being angry, is thrilled by what she sees on his canvas: "She kissed him with transports of affection, and assured him that she would not only intercede with his father to pardon him for having absented himself from school, but would go herself to the master, and beg that he might not be punished." Whatever the facts, there must be a degree of truth in these accounts of maternal support. That support fortified what Galt was much later to describe as "a persuasion that he was endowed by Heaven with a peculiar gift" in giving West a firm belief in himself, which would not waver for the next seventy years.[5]

Galt tells us that Indians gave the aspiring artist his first instruction in mixing colors, a story which we may be inclined to disbelieve. Concrete assistance in mastering the technicalities of his craft came from a distant cousin, Edward Penington, a young Philadelphia merchant.[6] Penington sent the boy paints, canvases, and engravings to copy. He also invited Benjamin to visit him in Philadelphia, and there West had his first encounter with a real artist, an Englishman named William Williams (1727–1791). In 1810 West wrote that he met Williams in 1747, a date that accords reasonably well with Galt's sequence of events.[7] Although Williams was himself only twenty years old at the time and hardly presented a model of professional success (indeed he never had much success and was to die a pauper), the meeting must have been of inestimable importance for the youth fresh from Chester County. Williams's pictures were probably the first actual paintings he ever saw, and Williams introduced him to the history of art by lending him books by Charles Alphonse du Fresnoy and Jonathan Richardson. These books were du Fresnoy's *De arte graphica*, in the translation of 1695 by John Dryden, which included a "short account of the most eminent painters both ancient and modern," and probably Richardson's *Account of Some of the Statues, Bas-Reliefs, Drawings and Pictures in Italy* of 1722. West read them as inspiring stories of artists' lives, rather than as theoretical treatises; he took them back to the country, where his parents read them as well; and the impression they made seems effectively to have settled what the nine-year-old boy's life's work would be. This early commitment and West's mother's encouragement of his devotion to art at the expense of schoolwork were to carry a price. In 1804 his wife told the artist Joseph Farington, "He was so devoted to drawing while a Child and a Youth, that every other part of his education was neglected,"[8] and her great-nephew, the writer Leigh Hunt, who was a frequent visitor in the West home in London, declared the artist "had received so careless, or so homely an education when a boy, that he could hardly read."[9] By 1747 West was sufficiently comfortable with books to be able to read du Fresnoy and Richardson, but by any conventional standard he remained woefully undereducated, and picturesque errors in grammar and spelling punctuate all his correspondence.

West's activities between 1747 and 1756 are difficult to track, but it seems certain that they included less and less formal schoolwork, and that he spent less and less time at his father's inn in Newtown Square. We know that he lived with his older sister Rachel and her husband in Philadelphia for some time during the 1750's and that a pair of juvenile pictures which have belonged to the Pennsylvania Hospital since 1818 were painted by West as over-mantels in a house in Strawberry Alley in Philadelphia, where he was said to have boarded when he was fifteen years old.[10] In 1805 West told Farington that he had been given some instruction as a boy in Philadelphia by a "Mr. Hide," a German artist who had previously been in London. "Mr. Hide" has been identified as John Valentine Haidt, a goldsmith, Moravian lay preacher, and painter, who came to America in 1754 to live in the Moravian community in Bethlehem, Pennsylvania.[11]

Immediately after his arrival he served as a substitute preacher in Philadelphia from June 1754 to September 1755, and West must have been instructed by him then.

Along with the two over-mantels from Strawberry Alley, the earliest paintings generally accepted as West's work are a pair of small portraits of the children of a neighbor in Chester County, traditionally said to have been painted about 1752.[12] He is recorded as having charged one guinea for a painting of a head in 1754, two guineas in 1755, three in 1756, four in 1758, five in January 1760, and prices double those for half-length figures. In 1756, and possibly starting in 1755, he spent several months painting portraits in Lancaster, Pennsylvania, sixty miles west of Philadelphia. The illness and death of his mother in the summer of 1756 brought his stay there to an abrupt end, but eight portraits painted at Lancaster and one picture of a historical subject, *The Death of Socrates* (cat. 2), are now known. According to Galt, his success there was so great "that it was with difficulty he could find time to satisfy the demands of his admirers."

In August 1756, following his mother's funeral, West "took his final departure" from his father's inn to live with his sister and brother-in-law in Philadelphia, where he continued to paint portraits. He also became a protégé of the Reverend William Smith, a classical scholar, Anglican minister, and moving figure in the cultural and intellectual life of Philadelphia in the 1750's. Smith, who was born in Scotland, had come to teach in Philadelphia in 1754 at the invitation of Benjamin Franklin. In 1755, at the age of twenty-eight, he became the first provost of the College of Philadelphia (now the University of Pennsylvania), which he was instrumental in founding. He visited Lancaster in 1756, evidently met West there, saw *The Death of Socrates*, and thereupon invited the young man to study with him in Philadelphia. West did not become a formally enrolled student in the College of Philadelphia, probably because he had to support himself by devoting his days to painting portraits. In the evenings, Smith undertook to acquaint him with classical literature and give him "a sketch of the taste and character of the spirit of antiquity, as would have all the effect of the regular education requisite to a painter." Smith did not subject West to "those grammatical exercises of language which are usually required from the young student of the classics," and which constituted the core of an eighteenth-century education. Nevertheless, if West was not enrolled in the College of Philadelphia, he became a member of Smith's small group of students socially. Galt lists four young men to whom Smith introduced him: Francis Hopkinson, Thomas Godfrey, Joseph Reed, and Jacob Duché. Hopkinson, who in 1757 received the first degree granted by the College of Philadelphia, was to become a poet, composer, and lawyer, and was in 1776 a signer of the Declaration of Independence. Godfrey was a poet and wrote the first American play to be performed professionally upon the stage. Reed became a member of the Continental

Cat. 2. *The Death of Socrates.* (ca. 1756)
Oil on canvas. 34 x 41 in. (86.4 x 104.2 cm.)
Private Collection

Congress, a revolutionary general, a statesman, and president of the trustees of his old school when it became the University of Pennsylvania. Duché entered the Anglican clergy and was chaplain of the Continental Congress, but had a change of heart in 1777 and spent the rest of his life as a loyalist exile in England. Thus West found himself in the midst of what must have been one of the most precocious and stimulating circles in the colonies.

In 1757 Smith founded *The American Magazine and Monthly Chronicle for the British Colonies*, to which Hopkinson, Duché, and Godfrey were contributors in verse, and to which West may have contributed as well by providing the design for the cover illustration (cat. 53). A painting by West also inspired a poem in the fifth issue of the magazine in February 1758, "Upon seeing the portrait of Miss **——** by Mr. West," and seven months later the magazine included ten more lines of fulsome praise of West concluding a verse by Hopkinson devoted to the itinerant portrait painter John Wollaston. The earlier poem was prefaced by a note stating that the Miss **——** of the portrait, the equally anonymous poet who signed himself "Lovelace," and the painter were all "natives of this place and very young," followed by another note which provided publicity rather than anonymity for the nineteen-year-old painter:

> We are glad of this opportunity of making known to the world, the name of so extraordinary a genius as Mr. West. He was born in Chester county in this province, and without the assistance of any master, has acquired such delicacy and correctness of expression in his paintings joined to such a laudable thirst of improvement, that we are persuaded, when he shall have obtained more experience and proper opportunities of viewing the productions of able masters, he will become truly eminent in his profession.

Since this note was probably written by Smith, it is not evidence of West's growing reputation. Rather, in introducing the artist and suggesting the route he should follow to gain eminence, it reflects Smith's role, not only as mentor to the "extraordinary genius," but also in promoting his career.

To see "the production of able masters" West would have to travel abroad, and his activity between 1757 and 1760 was directed in single-minded fashion to allow him to do so. In Galt's words, he adopted "a most rigid system of frugality." The early *Death of Socrates* was not followed by further experiments in history painting because only by responding to the established demand for portraits could West earn what he needed. When he had raised his prices as far as the local market would bear, he made a professional journey to New York. There, according to Galt, he raised them again, had much employment, and in eleven months saved enough money to pay for a short trip to Italy. There is, however, some question if he could have been in New York as long and could have been as productive as Galt

claims, since not a single work painted by him in New York has been identified. He probably went to New York sometime in 1759. While he was there, Provost Smith prepared his next step by arranging passage for him on a merchant ship sailing with a load of sugar from Philadelphia to Italy. West returned to Pennsylvania and set sail on the *Betty Sally* on April 12, 1760. At some point he had become engaged to marry Elizabeth Shewell (1741–1814), the daughter of a Philadelphia merchant. But art came first: "The marriage would have taken place then, but Mr. West could not think of sitting down for life in America, without first having had recourse to those means of improvement in his profession, which Europe only afforded."[13] So, following the example of his father who forty-five years before had abandoned a pregnant wife to come to America, he left, with a promise to return.

The *Betty Sally* arrived at Leghorn (or Livorno) on the coast of Tuscany on June 16. Armed with letters of introduction provided by Robert Rutherford, the English factor in Leghorn to whom the sugar had been sent, West went on to Rome a few weeks later. There he was immediately plunged into a world of milords on the Grand Tour, artists, and connoisseurs. He was the first American artist ever to have traveled to Italy, and he was, for many of his new acquaintances, the first living product from his remote continent they had encountered. In 1794 West described to the students of the Royal Academy schools in London how "most of the *Cognoscenti* in that grand Asylum of the Arts" accompanied him on an excursion to the Vatican to look at the *Apollo Belvedere* so they might see "how a native of America who could have no opportunity of contemplating the fine remains of antiquity would be affected by a view of the most perfect figure that Sculpture had produced."[14] West rose to the occasion by exclaiming "how like a Young *Mohock Warrior*!", thus satisfactorily shocking his distinguished audience by his irreverence. He redeemed himself with a description of the "strength, agility and grace" of the Mohawks, resulting from their healthy, outdoor pursuits.

Within six weeks of his arrival, West had met the leading painter of the emerging neoclassical movement, and the most admired artist then working in Rome, Anton Raphael Mengs, and had been advised by him about how to spend the rest of his time in Italy. What Mengs told West was to see everything worthy in Rome and make drawings of a few classical sculptures; visit Florence, Bologna, Parma, and Venice; then return to Rome to paint and exhibit a historical picture. West did exactly that, but because of bad health it was to take him three years. Mengs soon left Rome for a long sojourn at the Spanish court in Madrid, and West never saw him again after the summer of 1761, but the advice he received, "he never forgot, nor remembered without gratitude."[15]

Although West was to live to the age of eighty-one and was sufficiently hale and hearty to produce a huge painted

Cat. 4. *Anne, Countess of Northampton, and Her Daughter,*
Lady Elizabeth Compton. 1762
Oil on canvas. 51¼ x 41½ in. (130.2 x 105.5 cm.)
Bass Museum of Art: Gift of John and Johanna Bass, 63.32

oeuvre, poor health plagued his younger life. According to
Galt, he invented his own version of the camera obscura as
a boy in Philadelphia while confined to bed by a fever. In
1770 he was prevented from sending a major new painting
to the second exhibition of the Royal Academy because
sickness had deprived him of more than six months of
work. And, most significantly, disease dominated his three-
year stay in Italy. After less than six weeks in Rome in
1760, rheumatic pains brought on by the heat forced him
to return to Leghorn for several months of recuperation.
He went back to Rome in the winter, but had to leave in
the summer of 1761, retreating once again to Leghorn, then
moving to Florence where he underwent a series of opera-
tions on an infected ankle between November 1761 and
February 1762. He recovered sufficiently to work and travel
by the summer of 1762. Being afraid of the climate of
Rome, he set off on his tour of Bologna, Parma, and Venice,
and did not arrive back in Rome until January 1763, leaving
the city for good the following May. His shaky health, by
precluding any extended stay in Rome, precluded entering
into any regular course of academic study. Thus, while West
left Italy in 1763 armed with knowledge of "the productions

of able masters" that had been denied him in colonial
Pennsylvania, he did not (and never would) repair his early
lack of opportunity for professional instruction in drawing
and painting.

In Italy West did paint at least six copies after old masters—
the *Venus of Urbino* by Titian, the *Madonna and Child with
St. Jerome* by Correggio, and works by or ascribed to
Annibale Carracci, Domenichino, Guido Reni, and van
Dyck—and two copies after Mengs.[16] Most of the copies
were made for Chief Justice William Allen of Pennsylvania,
the wealthiest man in the colony, and for his brother-in-
law, Lieutenant-Governor James Hamilton. Judge Allen had
owned the load of sugar that gave West the opportunity to
travel in Italy. John Allen, his eldest son, and Joseph Shippen,
a relative who served as his agent, were West's shipmates.
Their reports from Italy of "Mr. West's Genius in the
painting way" and of his prolonged and expensive sickness
prompted Judge Allen and Governor Hamilton to advance
West £300 to be repaid by the copies. This money allowed
the artist to remain in Italy longer than he originally had
intended, while painting the copies provided not only his
prime occupation, but also a significant component (in place
of formal instruction) of his artistic education.

The patronage of Judge Allen and Governor Hamilton
was an embodiment of West's continuing ties to the Pennsylvania to which he intended to return in due course, and
the copies were dispatched to Philadelphia, where they were
seen and studied by other aspiring artists, including John
Singleton Copley on a visit there in 1771. West also painted
a few portraits in Italy including one of John Allen,[17] but
more portentously for his future career all his other Italian
portraits, either known or recorded, showed English sitters
(see cat. 4). In Venice in the autumn of 1762 he met the
librarian of King George III, Richard Dalton, who was on
a buying trip for the king. Dalton was chiefly in search of
works by old masters, such as the great collection of pictures
by Canaletto and other Venetian artists which he purchased
during the visit and which is still one of the glories of the
royal collection, but he offered West a royal commission
for a small painting. That picture, of *Cymon and Iphigenia*,
West painted in Rome in the winter and spring of 1763,
following the advice given him by Mengs in 1760 (the
subject based on literature—Boccaccio and Dryden—was
"historical" according to the loose usage of the eighteenth
century).[18] It did not in fact enter the royal collection and
has disappeared, but Robert Rutherford reported to Joseph
Shippen in June 1763 that it had been "much admired by
the Judges at Rome." By then, encouraged by Dalton, who
led him to expect further commissions from George III, and
by his other English friends, West was en route, via Paris,
to London. He arrived there on August 20, 1763.

It is evident from Rutherford's correspondence with
Shippen and from a letter from West to Shippen written in
London on September 1, 1763, that West had not originally
intended to visit England.[19] All accounts also indicated that

he still planned to return to Philadelphia and to his fiancée after a brief stay in "the mother country which we Americans are all so desirous to see, and which I would not but desire as much, or more, than Italy itself." By what seems an amazing stroke of fate, both Provost Smith and Chief Justice Allen were in London when he arrived. In the spring of 1764 West sent three paintings to the annual exhibition of the recently established Society of Artists, where they were widely noticed and he was dubbed "the American Raphael."[20] By May, when Smith left to return to Philadelphia, West had evidently, after consultation with Smith and Allen, made the decision to remain. Smith, once back in Philadelphia, did "every Thing he expected of me in that Affair,"[21] and on June 24 Elizabeth Shewell, accompanied by West's father and her cousin the painter Matthew Pratt, sailed for England. The long-postponed marriage took place in St. Martin-in-the-Fields on September 2. John West went off to live with Benjamin's half-brother Thomas, the son born almost fifty years previously whom he had never before seen. Pratt became West's first recorded American student.

Married, firmly settled in England, and beginning to be active as a teacher as well as artist, West was twenty-five years old in the summer of 1764. Apart from progress onward and upward to ever greater success and recognition, he did not stray for the rest of his long life from the path upon which he had now established himself. He continued to exhibit with the Society of Artists through 1768 and became a director of that body. In 1768 he was among the leaders of a group of artists who seceded from the Society to form a new and more effective organization, the Royal Academy of Arts, which held its first exhibition the following spring. He sent works to the Academy's annual exhibition every year but one from 1769 to 1819, and following the death of Sir Joshua Reynolds in 1792, he became the second president of the Academy. In December 1805, because of factional disputes, he resigned the office, but he resumed it again a year later and remained the Academy's president until his death, serving longer than any other artist in its history.

The patronage of George III promised to West by Richard Dalton did not instantly materialize, but by 1767 West had won the support of the Archbishop of York, the second highest prelate in the Church of England, and following the archbishop's introduction he received a commission from the king for a work which appeared in the first exhibition of the Royal Academy in 1769 (cat. 12). It was the first of some sixty pictures, many on a very large scale, which between 1768 and 1801 he would paint for George III. In 1772 he was appointed Historical Painter to the King; in 1791 he succeeded Dalton as Surveyor of the King's Pictures; and from 1780 to 1810 he received a stipend of £1,000 a year from the crown.

West gained popular recognition and a substantial income not only from his paintings, but also from reproductive prints after them. Prints also helped him achieve an international reputation and influence, although in America he had a more direct and powerful influence through teaching a steady stream of his younger compatriots, including students of such future eminence as Charles Willson Peale, Gilbert Stuart, and John Trumbull, who came to London for the sake of his tutelage.[22] In 1811 West achieved public recognition of another sort, as well as further income, when his large painting of *Christ Healing the Sick* (see cat. 69) was purchased for 3,000 guineas, a sum believed at the time to be the record amount received by an artist for one painting. He followed it with two even larger sequels, *Christ Rejected* (see cat. 52) and *Death on the Pale Horse* (see cat. 38). After his death, these two paintings became the centerpiece of a gallery devoted to his works which his sons built in the garden of his former home and operated as a commercial venture from 1821 to 1828.

After 1763 West left England only once, for a trip to Paris in 1802 during a lull in the Napoleonic wars. He lived in London in the vicinity of Leicester Square until 1775, then for the rest of his life at No. 14 Newman Street, north of Oxford Street, in a new house with a garden, at the rear of which he built a large skylit painting room. Mrs. West died in December 1814. He died on March 11, 1820. They had two sons: Raphael Lamar, born in April 1766, and Benjamin, born in August 1772. After the death of their mother, Benjamin, with his wife and son, came to live with and look after his father. Both sons worked as West's studio assistants, as did many of his pupils, including Trumbull and Stuart. Raphael had a brief career of his own as an artist, but in the words of the painter Charles Robert Leslie, who studied with West in 1811, he "possessed more talent than industry."[23] He started to exhibit at the Royal Academy in 1781, when he was fifteen years old, but ceased ten years later after an unsuccessful bid for election to associate membership. After West's death, despite the considerable fortune Raphael had been left, he ultimately had to apply to the Academy for charitable assistance.

West's progression from rural Chester County to the court of George III and presidency of the Royal Academy was a remarkable success story, no matter how much Galt was to embellish it. West certainly saw it as such, as his pictures of himself and his family show. In 1777 he sent a small group portrait of his family to that year's Royal Academy exhibition (cat. 17). It had been painted, or begun, five years earlier, shortly after the birth of his second son, Benjamin, who is seen as a baby on his mother's lap. John West, the artist's father, died in October 1776, and West probably exhibited the picture the following spring as a tribute, since the composition is focused upon him and his oldest son Thomas. Seated together and dressed in Quaker garb, they are far more carefully and precisely delineated than their companions; the thinly painted artist appears squeezed into the upper right corner as a compositional afterthought.

As a group portrait on a small scale, *The West Family* is a "conversation piece" in the manner of Johann Zoffany. Yet it is more than just a group portrait. It records the first

Cat. 17. *The West Family.* (ca. 1772)
Oil on canvas. 20½ x 26¼ in. (52.1 x 66.7 cm.)
Yale Center for British Art, New Haven, Connecticut:
Paul Mellon Collection

Cat. 8. *Jacob Blessing the Sons of Joseph.* 1766
Oil on canvas. 40 1/16 x 51 in. (101.8 x 129.6 cm.)
Allen Memorial Art Museum, Oberlin College:
R.T. Miller, Jr. Fund, 61.70
©Allen Memorial Art Museum

visit of West's father and half-brother to see the newest addition to the family and shows the two Quakers sitting "for a few minutes in silent meditation, which will soon be ended by the old man's taking off his hat and offering up a prayer for the mother and infant." That description comes from Charles Robert Leslie, who stated that West thought of the painting also as a depiction of the ages of man, thus giving the autobiographical content a more general allegorical dimension. It is also tempting to look for significance in the sharply bifurcated composition with mother and children in a setting of upholstered furniture, curtains, and sunlight on the left; men before a plain background on the right. But what is most conspicuous is the contrast between West in curled wig and elegant dressing gown, palette in hand, and his father, over whose chair he leans. Leaning over his mother's chair on the opposite side of the composition, Raphael, aged six, echoes *his* father's visible rejection of the sober restraint in pose and dress of the two older men.

The West Family was engraved in 1779 and via the engraving became one of West's most popular works. Leslie, who as a nineteenth-century painter of small-scale genre subjects had little use for West's grander efforts, called it his most original picture. On the other hand, a contemporary critic in 1777 complained that in exhibiting his own family in such a manner the artist was singing his own praises: "he should no more publish this to the world, than a poet should a commendatory poem on his own family." West, nevertheless, did display his family to the English public frequently in straightforward portraits and as models for figures in pictures of other subjects. Shortly before he began *The West Family* he used likenesses of John West and Thomas West for two of the Quaker companions of the founder of Pennsylvania in *Penn's Treaty with the Indians* (cat. 15). They, of course, could not have been present at a ceremony that was supposed to have taken place in 1682, but in West's mind they must have been appropriate substitutes for the Quakers who had been there, among them, purportedly, his own maternal grandfather Thomas Pearson.

The subject of *Penn's Treaty* has a geographical and historical relevance to West's own background that hardly requires spelling out. Even the large elm tree under which the meeting takes place was described by West as one "to which I well remember, about the year 1755, when a boy, often resorting with my school-fellows." No other historical subject that he undertook presented West content of such explicitly personal concern, but many of his works can be interpreted as implicitly referring to developments in his own life. *Jacob Blessing the Sons of Joseph* (cat. 8) shows a biblical subject, from Genesis 48. It also shows a successful youngest child from a large family rejoined by his father in a foreign land. Probably painted in 1766, two years after John West had come to England, and shortly after the birth of Raphael West on April 8 of that year, it depicts an Old Testament scene that West would virtually recreate, after

the birth of his second son, in the contemporary, personal, and Quaker idiom of *The West Family*.

West manifested his affection for his first-born child in several compositions showing Mrs. West with Raphael in her arms, painted shortly before 1770 (cats. 14 and 57), and in a companion portrait of himself at work with Raphael looking over his shoulder, painted a few years later (cat. 60). He exhibited a version (probably cat. 14) of the picture of Raphael with his mother at the Royal Academy in 1770 simply as "a portrait of a mother and child" without further identification of the sitters (as he subsequently exhibited *The*

Cat. 14. *Mrs. West with Raphael West.* (ca. 1770)
Oil on canvas. 36 in. diameter (91.5 cm. diameter)
Marriner S. Eccles Foundation for the Marriner S. Eccles
Masterwork Collection, Utah Museum of Fine Arts,
Salt Lake City

West Family as "A small picture of a family"), but visitors to the exhibition had no difficulty in determining who they were. If personal meaning insinuated itself into religious subject matter in *Jacob Blessing the Sons of Joseph*, religious overtones are equally prominent in these double portraits. The round, tondo, shapes recall those of Renaissance devotional images, and the composition of the artist's wife with her son in her arms depends directly on the Madonnas of Raphael, specifically the *Madonna della Sedia* in the Pitti Palace in Florence, which West had studied at first hand in 1762. Such overt borrowing constitutes an act of homage to the master towards whom West made obeisance in another fashion when naming his son. As do pictures of mothers

Cat. 40. *Raphael and Benjamin West, Sons of the Artist.* (1796)
Oil on canvas. 35¼ x 28¼ in. (89.6 x 71.8 cm.)
The Nelson-Atkins Museum of Art, Kansas City, Missouri
(Gift of the Laura Nelson Kirkwood Residuary Trust)
© 1978 William Rockhill Nelson Trust

and children by many artists, it also suggests West's equation of his subjects with those of Raphael, projecting a quasi-divine aura around mother and son.

Benjamin Jr., who came second, did not receive the same doting attention as his older brother. His birth was celebrated in *The West Family*, but he is recorded otherwise only as being a subject in three portraits all shared with Raphael. Cat. 40 was the third of those joint portraits, painted in 1796 when Raphael was thirty years old and Benjamin twenty-four. West painted the picture as an experiment in the Venetian Secret (which is discussed on pp. 94–97), and that fact reminds us of a reason, apart from affection, love, or pride, for artists to paint members of their families. When models are required, the family is there, not only available, but free. Raphael must be the figure in front in the double portrait, ahead of and more assertive than his withdrawn younger brother. No longer infant objects of semi-religious revery, as grown-up men Raphael and Benjamin appear to be tragi-romantic characters half lost in shadow. In actual life they were tragic figures who could not escape the shadow of their famous father.

Every known likeness by West of his wife and of his sons shows at least two people. He depicted them not individually, as individuals, but collectively, as members of his family. He did, on the other hand, frequently paint himself, apart from them, recording his changing appearance and celebrating his changing status in life. The *Self-Portrait* belonging to The Baltimore Museum of Art (cat. 24) shows the painter of *The Death of General Wolfe* (cat. 13), the picture which more than any other established his reputation. In his left hand he holds what appears to be a drawing, but may have been intended to represent a marked proof of the engraving by William Woollett after the painting (cat. 61), which was published on January 1, 1776, and had even greater popular impact. The large beaver hat and the artist's gaze from the corner of his eye also bring to mind another work of art, a well-known *Self-Portrait* by Rubens in the English royal collection, and we are probably safe in believing that they convey some identification with that most worldly and successful of artists. By the mid-1770's West probably did think of himself at moments as another Rubens, not without a modicum of historical justification. Like West, Rubens was not a native Englishman, yet he did work briefly in England and was knighted by Charles I. His *Self-Portrait* was commissioned by Charles I, and West must have known it well from visits to Buckingham House, in conjunction with his commissions from George III. Following his appointment as Historical Painter to the King in 1772, he could hardly have failed to think of himself analogously as artist and courtier. While still in his thirties and after little more than a decade in England, he had achieved more than sufficient success to shed all traces of the aspiring artist struggling to make his way. Turning to look at us, his face half concealed in shadow, he appears more aware of himself and certainly more complex as a

Cat. 60. *Self-Portrait with Raphael West.* 1775
Mezzotint by Valentine Green
Sheet: 15⁷⁄₁₆ x 11 in. (392 x 28 mm.)
The Baltimore Museum of Art: Garrett Collection
(BMA 1946.112.10158)

person in the Baltimore picture than does the artist-father in the self-portrait with Raphael looking over his shoulder painted a few years before (cat. 60). Stylistically, the greater assurance of handling and complication of composition reflect West's attention to Rubens and anticipate the increasingly baroque quality of his art in the later 1770's and the 1780's. However, the direct, uncomplicated technique of painting with pronounced and clear brushstrokes is the antithesis of Rubens's glazes and probably owes something to the example of John Singleton Copley, who arrived in England from Boston in 1774.

The *Self-Portrait* from the Royal Academy (cat. 37) is dated 1792, the year in which West was elected the Academy's president, and it portrays the artist seated in the president's chair, looking out at us with the assurance of a successful and responsible executive. Papers, a magnifying glass, and a quill pen establish that he is at his desk doing the Academy's work. Somerset House, the home of the Academy, is in the background, and appropriately, the part of Somerset House that we are shown is the southern part adjacent to the Thames, as it would have been seen across

Cat. 37. *Self-Portrait.* (1792)
Oil on panel. 40 x 52 in. (101.6 x 132.1 cm.)
The Royal Academy of Arts, London
©Royal Academy of Arts

the courtyard from the northern block on the Strand, which housed the Academy. The piece of sculpture on the right is a cast of the antique *Belvedere Torso* in the Vatican, of which there was and is a cast in the Royal Academy. More than simply a work admired by West, the *Torso* was an academic icon because of Michelangelo's admiration (in the eighteenth century the *Torso* was even nicknamed "the school of Michelangelo"), and because, as claimed by Reynolds in his tenth discourse, the perfection of the "science of abstract form" it exemplified could only be appreciated after long study. The titles on two of the books stacked before it, *History of Greece* and *History of England*, remind us of the Academy's raison d'être as a learned institution, and recall the sources for many of West's own paintings, thus proclaiming the learned artist and painter of lofty historical subjects whom we see in the portrait as the ideal representative of the standards the Academy existed to uphold.

The inclusion of paper, books, sculpture, and architecture in a portrait to make a statement about the sitter has a long history and considerable precedent in works by West (for example cat. 9). Nevertheless, the prototype uppermost in his mind as he depicted himself as president of the Royal Academy must have been Reynolds's well-known portrait of himself wearing academic robes, holding his discourses, and watched over by a bust of Michelangelo. West's picture is linked more explicitly than Reynolds's with the Academy by the presence of Somerset House in the background (and the composition seems to have been stretched horizontally to make room for it), but this detail echoes a companion portrait by Reynolds to the one of himself. That portrait shows Sir William Chambers, the Academy's treasurer and the architect of Somerset House, and includes a view of the Strand facade of his new building in the background. Reynolds presented the portraits of Chambers and himself to the Academy to hang in its premises in Somerset House,[24] which would seem to have been the obvious destination of West's portrait of himself as well, but West did not give it. It would have been in character for him to have expected his fellow artists to buy it as a mark of respect. However, the painting remained in his possession until his death and was bought in the sale of his estate in 1829 by a private collector, who then gave it to the Academy.

We might think that West would have felt honored by the recognition implied in his election as president of the Royal Academy, but he seems to have considered it only his due. Upon his election, he was offered a knighthood, following the precedent of the knighthood conferred on the Academy's first president, Sir Joshua Reynolds (which would be followed for all presidents after West). He declined it because, as quoted by Galt, "he really thought he had already earned by his pencil more eminence than could be conferred on him by that rank."[25] This was not self-denial based on humility, principle, or lingering Quaker convictions, but an assertion that his stature as an artist called for a higher rank: for a hereditary peerage. His self-esteem was inevitably found offensive by many of his contemporaries and was considered ridiculous by those who did not share his appreciation of his own work. His self-portraits have been criticized as images of vanity and pomposity; more charitably it could be said that pride and self-satisfaction radiate from West's likenesses of himself because he believed in his own genius and in the quality and significance of the works he produced. His view of himself was affectionately encapsulated by his great-nephew Leigh Hunt in an account of boyhood visits to West's painting room, where he generally found "the mild and quiet artist at his work; happy, for he thought himself immortal."[26]

Cat. 5. *The Cricketers.* (1763?)
Oil on canvas. 40 x 50 in. (101.6 x 127 cm.)
Private Collection

2. From the New World to the Old

The first significant group of West's works that has come down to us stems from a visit that he paid to Lancaster, Pennsylvania, probably in 1755 and 1756. It is possible that he went to Lancaster more than once, but his eight known portraits of Lancaster sitters have enough in common to suggest that they were all painted during one relatively brief period. Galt tells us that he made his trip to paint portraits of the family of the attorney George Ross (cat. 1) and that their success led to further commissions. Ross (1730–1779), the son of an Anglican minister, was to be a member of the Continental Congress, a signer of the Declaration of Independence, and a judge. West painted him when he was twenty-five or, at the most, twenty-six years old. A companion portrait of his wife belongs, like cat. 1 to Franklin and Marshall College in Lancaster, and a portrait of his sister still belongs to her descendants.[1]

Before West went to Lancaster, he had had some personal contact with two artists: William Williams and John Valentine Haidt,[2] but how much he could have learned from either is a question. He may not yet have seen any actual European paintings, assuredly none of any real quality, but he had seen and copied engravings, and he must have seen portraits painted by Gustavus Hesselius and his son John Hesselius, who lived and worked on and off in Philadelphia, and by Robert Feke, who visited Philadelphia in 1746 and 1749. Feke had a strong impact on the early works of John Hesselius, who started to paint around 1749, and, directly or indirectly via Hesselius, he was probably the chief model for West's Lancaster portraits. That is evident in the portrait of Mrs. Ross, whose pose recalls those of Feke's *Mrs. Tench Francis* and other portraits painted by him in Philadelphia.[3] The *George Ross* is not as obviously related to any single prototype, but the simply defined composition and almost geometric clarity of line do show an affinity with Feke. What is most distinctive is the frontal pose, which gives the lawyer a friendly openness and suggests that the artist was trying to devise his own way of delineating his subject instead of relying upon formulae that he could learn from other artists. The painting shows conspicuous technical limitations, but, in light of the young artist's lack of experience, a remarkable degree of ambition in scale and composition. If West could not make Ross's face more than an inexpressive mask, he conceived of his portrait as more than a face and showed Ross surrounded by a column, some furniture, and books. The column is a conventional device (would there have been such columns in mid-eighteenth-century Lancaster?), and the inclusion of books was hardly unconventional. Yet West inscribed titles, which are now almost entirely illegible, on the books, so they do appear to represent actual books belonging to Ross, and their presence is in keeping with what we know about him: in 1755 he was one of the citizens of Lancaster who subscribed to employ a Latin schoolmaster, and he was to be one of the first directors of the library in Lancaster founded in 1759. While West may not yet have been capable of telling us very much about the sitter's physical appearance, the portrait does tell us something about his concerns.

Another of West's Lancaster subjects who took an interest in the library was a gunsmith named William Henry in whose house it was situated from 1766 to 1776. While West was painting Henry and his wife, Henry told him that he was wasting his time on portraits and proposed that he paint a historical subject. The result was *The Death of Socrates* (cat. 2), the artist's first venture into what would be the central activity of his mature life. West learned the story of Socrates drinking hemlock from the ten-volume *Ancient History* of Charles Rollin published in the 1730's, which Henry had in his library, and he based his composition on the frontispiece to volume four, an engraving of the subject after a design by the French artist Hubert Gravelot (fig. 1). One of Henry's workers posed for the half-naked slave standing over Socrates in the center of the picture.

Although West painstakingly copied many of his details from the frontispiece, his painting is not a copy, but

Cat. 1. *George Ross.* (ca. 1755–1756)
Oil on canvas. 42½ x 33½ in. (108 x 85.1 cm.)
College Collections, Gift of Mrs. George Ross Eshleman,
Franklin and Marshall College, Lancaster, Pennsylvania

portraits, such as the *George Ross*. Nevertheless, the novelty of the undertaking made *The Death of Socrates* the most ambitious and interesting picture produced in colonial America, one whose significance in his own career West acknowledged well before he started to tell the story of his early life to Galt. In his account, it was important not because it was his first history painting, but because the use of Henry's workman as a model gave him "the disposition to copy nature." Despite being studied from a living model, the semi-nude slave carries none of the anatomical conviction that he might have displayed if West had confined himself to copying the engraving. His pose is roughly that of Gravelot's corresponding figure, but Gravelot's slave is not half-nude; he wears a ragged garment that covers his

Fig. 1. Hubert Gravelot (French, 1699–1773)
The Death of Socrates. 1739
Engraving by J.P. LeBas. 5½ x 3⅛ in. (135 x 79 mm.)
Photograph courtesy Allen Staley

something quite different from its source. Whereas Gravelot's composition is vertical, West's is horizontal, expanded in width to accommodate more than twice as many figures, a more elaborate architectural setting, and a cloud-streaked sky in the background. The composition has become symmetrical with the fatal cup of hemlock at the center and a group of soldiers added on one side to balance Socrates's distressed friends, who have been moved to the other. While Gravelot's actors are seen before and behind one another in a spatially convincing setting, West's are placed side by side in a more primitive two-dimensional arrangement. The additional architecture, delineated stone by stone, demonstrates that West had not mastered the intricacies of one-point perspective and creates a screen across the picture helping to flatten the composition.

The painting is not only more primitive than Gravelot's engraving (as we of course should expect), but also, because of the novelty of the undertaking and the more complex challenge it entailed, it makes us more aware of the artist's inexperience and inabilities than do his contemporaneous shoulders and the rib cage that is so unconvincingly rendered by West. The slave in the frontispiece hands Socrates the cup with his right hand and points to it with his left. In West's painting his right hand hangs idly at his side, and with his left he holds up his oddly conical loincloth. This detail is evidence that West did copy the slave from a real, but inexperienced model, who was compelled to keep whatever approximation of classical drapery West and Henry had wrapped around him from falling down. Such a figure is not a triumph of anatomy, historical understanding, or grace, but he does embody West's effort, after rejecting the easy solution of copying, to work through things on his own.

West's Socrates does not depart radically from Gravelot's, but instead of taking the cup from the slave, he holds it before his mouth, as if about to drink. The focus in Gravelot is on the physical act. In West there is no action; the two main actors are as static as statues, and the focus is upon Socrates's poignantly upturned eyes. Consequently, the picture is not the inspiring scene of heroic or philosophical self-sacrifice for the sake of principles which we might reasonably expect a painting of the death of Socrates to be, but a touching depiction of the pathos of a docile little old man accepting his fate: not a very sophisticated reading of the story, but a visibly deeply-felt one.

Before leaving America, West followed *The Death of Socrates* with only one further historical painting, which was said to have been destroyed in a fire before 1840. However, a composition, which is known but presents questions of attribution, might also be looked upon as a sequel. That is the illustration that appeared on the covers of Provost Smith's

Cat. 53. *Praevalebit Aequior.* (ca. 1757)
Attributed to Benjamin West
Sheet: 8 x 5 in. (203 x 127 mm.)
Rare Books Room, Library of Congress, Washington, D.C.

American Magazine from October 1757 to October 1758 (cat. 53). Inscribed *Praevalebit Aequior* ("the more equitable will prevail"), it shows two figures in European dress, evidently English and French, standing on either side of a scantily clad American Indian, who leans upon a flintlock musket.[4] The Englishman, on the Indian's right, proffers a book; the Frenchman, opposite, a hatchet or tomahawk. In 1757, in a time of armed conflict between England and France in North America (the French and Indian or Seven Years' War), the allegorical message of this confrontation would not have required much explanation. The image is an adaptation of the traditional subject of Hercules at the crossroads choosing between Virtue and Vice, transformed to embody a topical meaning. The pose of the Indian leaning on his gun appears to have been derived from that of Hercules leaning on his club in an engraving of the *Choice of Hercules* after the Neapolitan painter Paolo de Matteis, which served to illustrate a well-known treatise on the subject by the third Earl of Shaftesbury, and which, because of that literary association, was probably in Provost Smith's library. Such reliance upon a print echoes West's procedure in *The Death of Socrates*, while the transformation of subject and composition to serve up-to-date purposes is prophetic of his future practices, but, unfortunately, the quality of the actual print is too crude to allow us to say much more, or even to be confident that it is by West. Provost Smith had been inspired by sight of *The Death of Socrates* in 1756 to invite West to study with him, and it seems likely enough that he would have asked his protégé to design the cover of the periodical he started the following year, but West was not the only artist in his circle. Thomas Godfrey was described by Smith in *The American Magazine* as being devoted to the muses of both poetry and painting, and a poem by Godfrey in the issue of October 1758 contained a reference to "the expressive art of G——." After Godfrey's death, Smith wrote that G—— was "Mr. John Green, an ingenious Portrait Painter, a particular friend of Mr. Godfrey's."[5] He was also a friend of West. A drawing of Green holding a palette and brushes is in a sketchbook used by West in Philadelphia (The Historical Society of Pennsylvania), and a letter written by West to Green in 1771 laments their twelve-year separation after "so many years Friendship had subsisted between us in America."[6] Until we know more about Green, we cannot ascribe *The American Magazine* cover to West simply on the basis of his place in Smith's circle, nor can we be absolutely sure about the attribution to West of any portrait from this period.

None of the portraits traditionally believed to have been painted by West in Philadelphia after 1756 is signed or dated or firmly documented on other grounds. In September 1758 Francis Hopkinson linked his name with that of the peripatetic English-born portrait painter John Wollaston in a "Verses inscribed to Mr. Wollaston" in *The American Magazine*, and the portrait of *Elizabeth Peel* (cat. 3), showing a subject about whom we know next to nothing, demonstrates

Cat. 3. *Elizabeth Peel.* (ca. 1757–1758)
Oil on canvas. 47⅛ x 34⅜ in. (119.7 x 87.3 cm.)
Pennsylvania Academy of the Fine Arts, Philadelphia:
Gift of John Frederick Lewis

that the artist did look at Wollaston's portraits, such as that of Margaret Oswald (National Trust, Cliveden, Germantown, Pennsylvania),[7] presumably painted on a visit to Philadelphia in 1758. West copied the motif of holding a basket of flowers, the pose, the patterns of highlight and shadow to indicate shimmering satin, and the manner of allowing the face to be dominated by strongly modeled lips and large almond-shaped eyes. Hopkinson had instructed him in verse:

Hail sacred Genius! may'st thou ever tread,
The pleasing path your Wollaston has lead.
Let his just precepts all your works refine,
Copy each grace, and learn like him to shine.

Since that is what the *Elizabeth Peel* shows West doing, the portrait seems to demonstrate that he took the poet's message to heart, but it is perhaps more likely that Hopkinson's words, instead of instructing, were really reporting on West's current endeavors. In the previous February, the anonymous "Lovelace" in "Upon seeing the Portrait of Miss **——** by Mr. West" had contrasted the actual Miss **——** with Guido Reni's ability to "turn and animate" a face:

The easy attitude, the graceful dress,
The *soft expression* of the *perfect whole,*
Both *Guido's* judgment and his skill confess,
Informing canvas with a living soul.

There is no claim that West, whose name does not appear in the poem proper, possessed such judgment and skill, but we must assume that the qualities ascribed to Guido were those to which he aspired, or was being urged to aspire by the Reverend Smith. And it is in precisely these qualities, despite its deficiencies otherwise, that *Elizabeth Peel* does show progress from the frozen poses and expressionless faces of the Lancaster portraits. It is conventional and imitative of a model hardly worthy of the respect implied by imitation, whereas the *George Ross* and other Lancaster pictures display an unself-conscious and unsophisticated directness that allows us to understand the promise that Provost Smith and William Henry found in West. But to be more than a provincial limner, West had to break free from the ingenuous incompetence that the Lancaster pictures exude with such potent charm. To do so, he needed to view "the productions of able masters," as Smith wrote in February 1758. That Wollaston, who was himself little more than a marginally competent imitator of Thomas Hudson and other English artists active in the 1740's, had so great an impact upon him is evidence of how limited the opportunity to see anything in Philadelphia in the middle years of the eighteenth century had to be. In 1758 Wollaston was the most "able" master whose works West had yet seen.

Two years later, West arrived in Italy and entered another world. Since he was there to learn, not to produce, the output from his Italian sojourn was relatively small, but he did continue occasionally to paint portraits. His first painting done in Italy, within six weeks of his arrival, was a portrait that is lost but is the subject of a long anecdote by Galt:[8] West undertook it to show to Mengs as a demonstration of his abilities and it was sufficiently successful to fool the connoisseurs of Rome into believing that it was by Mengs. Since it is inconceivable that any of them could have believed that Mengs might produce work resembling *Elizabeth Peel* or anything else that West painted in Pennsylvania, the story, if true, is evidence of how rapidly and effectively he managed to shuck off the provincial limitations of his American style by turning to the new models Italy presented to him. Most of his known Italian portraits are as firmly in the manner of Mengs as the American ones of a year or two before are in the manner of Wollaston.[9] In them he substituted imitation of one successful practicing artist for another without looking beyond a contemporary frame of reference. But Italy offered more, and in one portrait, depicting the Countess of Northampton and her infant daughter (cat. 4), he took the step of incorporating lessons learned from earlier art into contemporary portraits.

West painted the countess and her child in Venice in the autumn of 1762. She was the daughter of the Duke of Beaufort and wife of the seventh Earl of Northampton, who had been appointed English Ambassador to Venice the previous August, but whose embassy was soon to be cut short by a double tragedy. The countess, who was twenty-one years old when West painted her, died of consumption the following May, and her husband died of the same disease five months later. Their orphaned two-year old daughter, the Lady Elizabeth Compton, survived and is the subject of a magnificent full-length portrait by Reynolds painted in 1781 and now in the National Gallery in Washington. She subsequently became Countess of Burlington.

West went to Venice in 1762 after a stay of several months in Florence and brief visits to Bologna and Parma. In Florence he had seen the *Madonna del Granduca* and *Madonna della Sedia* by Raphael in the Pitti Palace, and it is those two pictures, particularly the latter, that the portrait of the countess and her daughter most recalls. In this instance, West did more than study an old master in order to teach himself how to paint better pictures or, more specifically, to discover a way of combining the two figures of mother and child harmoniously in one picture, something he had not attempted previously; he utilized the language of Raphael's devotional images for a secular portrait in a manner that demands recognition. Robert Rutherford, the agent in Leghorn, in a letter written to Joseph Shippen reporting on West's activities described the picture as "the Ambassador's Lady in the Character of a Madonna, with her Child in her Arms, which gained great applause." A few years later West would paint his own wife in the same character in cat. 14 quoting from the same sources. He never actually copied the *Madonna della Sedia*, but a copy painted by a former student, John Downman, hung in his studio in London in later years, and it in turn was copied by subsequent students including John Trumbull and Thomas Sully.

We can assume that the earl paid for the portrait of his wife and child (according to Rutherford, West received fifty *zecchini* for it). The picture is thus a tangible product of the patronage of the English aristocracy which West attracted in Italy, and which would help to attract him to England. There, during his first ten years, commissions for portraits of the gentry and aristocracy provided his main income. In addition he painted Americans. In Italy he had no recorded encounters with his compatriots apart from John Allen and Joseph Shippen, with whom he had traveled, but England was full of them. Chief Justice Allen and Provost Smith were there when he arrived; Governor Hamilton came in 1765; Francis Hopkinson in 1766; John Green in 1774; and so on. Among his first English works were a portrait of Smith; portraits of Allen, his daughter, and one of his sons;[10] and a group portrait, of two Allen sons and three American friends, generally known as *The Cricketers* (cat. 5). The Allen brothers, Andrew (1740–1825) and James (1742–1778), were in England to study law at the Middle Temple in

London. Their three companions in *The Cricketers*, Ralph Wormeley (1745–1806) from Virginia, and Ralph Izard (1741/2–1804) and Arthur Middleton (1742–1787), both from Charleston, South Carolina, were students at Cambridge. The setting has traditionally been identified as Cambridge, with the river Cam, upon which we see pleasure boats and swans, flowing across the background. Arthur Middleton returned to Charleston in December 1763; so West must have at least commenced the picture by then, while the cricket bats and comfortable outdoor setting suggest that the season is summer or early fall.

The Cricketers belongs to a descendant of Andrew Allen, Justice Allen's second son (John, West's shipmate in 1760, was the first), who stands at the center of the picture. West painted a second version of the composition for Ralph Izard, who is the tall figure dressed in red, cricket bat in hand and hat on head, and he may have repeated it for the other sitters as well. If so, their pictures have not surfaced, and, in light of their subordinate positions, they might have been less eager to pay for a picture than Andrew Allen (or his father) and Izard. In 1763 Wormeley had Robert Edge Pine paint his portrait in academic robes before his Cambridge college (Virginia Historical Society, Richmond). In 1770 Middleton was back in England and was painted by West in a triple portrait together with his wife (a cousin of Ralph Izard) and their newborn son.[11] At about the same time West painted three further portraits of other members of the Middleton family.[12] Izard also returned to Europe with his bride, and in Rome in 1775 they sat for a memorable double portrait by Copley (Museum of Fine Arts, Boston).

A group portrait with full-length figures on a small scale such as *The Cricketers* is known as a conversation piece, a distinctly English genre, which flourished in the eighteenth century (*The West Family*, cat. 17, is a later example). West's adoption of the mode immediately upon his arrival in England would seem to be yet another nimble response to new stimuli, but this time he did not have to be quite as nimble as we might suppose, as he had seen English conversation pieces in Italy. During precisely the years he was there, the English painter Nathaniel Dance was painting similar small group portraits of their joint friends and patrons, young English milords, standing and sitting before the Colosseum and other monuments of Rome. Just as the Englishmen depicted by Dance were on their Grand Tours to the navel of European civilization, the Americans shown by West were on equivalent pilgrimages back to the mother country, the center of the world as seen from the colonies. The messages of youthful adventure and camaraderie, to be cherished during long adult lives after returning home, are the same, but events unforeseen in 1763 prevented the Americans from recalling this happy moment in untroubled tranquility. Ralph Izard and Arthur Middleton were to become members of the Continental Congress, and supporters of the American Revolution, but the Allen family remained loyal to Britain. James Allen died in 1778. Andrew,

General Hon.ᵇˡᵉ Robert Monckton.

Cat. 7. *Lieutenant General the Honorable Robert Monckton.*
(ca. 1764)
Oil on canvas. 94½ x 68⅜ in. (240.1 x 173.7 cm.)
The Descendants of the 8th Viscount Galway

who also was elected to the Continental Congress, opposed the Declaration of Independence, had his property confiscated in 1778, and spent the rest of his life exiled from his native land.

Within a year of his arrival in England, West also painted his first life-size full-length portrait, of *General Robert Monckton*, which he exhibited in the spring of 1764 (cat. 7). Monckton (1726–1782) came from an aristocratic family—he was the son of the first Viscount Galway and grandson of the second Duke of Rutland—but he also had an impressive military career in the American colonies. In 1759 he was second in command to General Wolfe at Quebec (see cat. 13). In 1760 he commanded the British forces in Pennsylvania, and in 1761 he was appointed governor of New York. In 1762, he led a successful expedition against the French in Martinique. He returned to England in the summer of 1763, shortly after West's arrival there. His path does not seem to have crossed West's in America, but Pennsylvania connections induced him to seek out the young artist in London. He knew or knew of West's older brother, Samuel West, who had been a captain in the Pennsylvania militia serving with the British in the French and Indian War, and by dint of his position, he must have known Chief Justice Allen and Provost Smith. West's portrait shows a cannon and tent in the foreground, red-coated troops in the middle distance, and a tropical town engulfed in flame beyond. Since Monckton holds a plan of Martinique, the painting unmistakably celebrates his recent victory there.

Such a depiction of a military officer was hardly novel. Before West painted him, Monckton had been portrayed in uniform with Quebec in the background by Thomas Hudson. But West's Monckton—stepping forward, head turned, arm outstretched and finger pointing, as if giving an order—is active, while Hudson's simply stands posing for his picture. Behind West's work there is a fundamentally different conception of portraiture, which he derived from a younger, more innovative, and better artist than Hudson (though one who had started as Hudson's pupil): Joshua Reynolds. We do not know precisely when West first met Reynolds, but in the spring of 1764 Reynolds saw and admired West's *Monckton* and advised him to exhibit it. When West called on Reynolds, he would have seen in his studio two full-length portraits of military officers dramatically recorded in moments of portentous action: Captain Richard Orme, carrying dispatches and about to mount his horse (National Gallery, London), and Commodore Augustus Keppel, striding along a stormy shore after a shipwreck (National Maritime Museum, Greenwich).[13] The former would have had a special attraction for West, because Orme had served as aide-de-camp to General Braddock in Pennsylvania in 1755, but the latter is a closer prototype in pose for West's picture. For that, West did not even need to have seen the picture itself (although he probably had) before beginning his own, as it had been engraved in 1759 and was Reynolds's most famous early work.

Cat. 54. *Savage Warrior Taking Leave of His Family.* 1763
Engraving by Francesco Bartolozzi
Sheet: 5¹³⁄₁₆ x 3¹¹⁄₁₆ in. (147 x 94 mm.)
Rare Book and Manuscript Library, Columbia University

General Monckton's striding pose and outstretched arm, like Commodore Keppel's, echo the *Apollo Belvedere*. Whether West consciously felt that he was utilizing a reminiscence of the *Apollo* in the portrayal of a contemporary man in contemporary uniform can probably never be determined. His portrait does not show the general "in the Character of an Apollo" in the manner that his portrait of the Countess of Northampton shows its subject "in the Character of a Madonna," and one would imagine that, while painting his first full-length portrait, West thought more about earlier full-length portraits, such as Reynolds's, than about ancient sculpture. Nevertheless, Monckton's pose also recalls the pose of one of West's own earlier figures, which inevitably does bring the *Apollo Belvedere* to mind because of West's remark about the Mohawk warrior quoted on p. 16. That figure is the *Savage Warrior* (see cat. 54), which he was asked

Cat. 55. *Indians Giving a Talk to Colonel Bouquet in a Conference at a Council Fire, near his Camp on the Banks of Muskingum in North America in Oct. 1764.* (1766)
Engraving by Charles Grignion
Sheet: 10 x 8½ in. (254 x 216 mm.)
Rare Books Room, Library of Congress, Washington, D.C.

to paint in September 1760, only a couple of months after first seeing the *Apollo*.

The request came in a letter from Joseph Shippen on behalf of the English Resident at Venice, where Shippen and John Allen had traveled in July when West went to Rome. The Resident had commissioned a picture or pictures of the four parts of the globe, which, according to Shippen, the unnamed Venetian artist was unable to finish because of his ignorance of the dress of American Indians. Since the subject of the four continents was popular in the eighteenth century—Tiepolo's ceiling of the staircase of the Residenz at Würzburg of a decade earlier is the most famous example— one suspects that the artist, who could have repeated the picturesque formulae that served Tiepolo and others, was not at a genuine impasse, and that the request was motivated by desire to create an opportunity for West. He fulfilled it in Leghorn in the autumn and winter of 1760–1761. The Venetian *Four Continents* has not been identified, but, before West left Italy, his painting also served as the basis of an engraving by Francesco Bartolozzi published as the frontis-

piece of an Italian translation of Edmund Burke's history of the European settlement of America (cat. 54).

West's Indian is full-length, but not life-sized (Shippen asked for a figure eighteen inches high). He is not a portrait, since he represents a type rather than an individual and was painted from memory rather than an actual sitter. Nevertheless, as a warrior carrying his weapon, he looks forward iconographically as well as in pose, to West's subsequent portrait of a warrior, General Monckton, carrying the most useful weapon of an officer of his rank, a map. As a savage he looks back to the Indian on the cover of *The American Magazine*, and, as a half-nude figure, to the half-nude slave in *The Death of Socrates* of 1756. In relation to either of those works (or any other work done by the artist prior to July 1760) he shows an amazing advance in the understanding of anatomy and the articulation of movement. The print may have been substantially helped by Bartolozzi, who was an experienced draughtsman, but we must credit West with coming a long way in the short time since his arrival in Italy, and the explanation for his progress lies in his first sight of art based upon the human body, classical sculpture. The connection of the *Savage Warrior* with classical sculpture is also thematic. In 1755 in *Thoughts on the Imitation of Greek Works in Painting and Sculpture*, Johann Winckelmann explained the ideal beauty of classical art as the expression of the healthy, natural lives of the ancient Greeks by drawing a modern analogy: ". . . Behold the swift Indian outstripping in pursuit the hart: how briskly his juices circulate! how flexible, how elastic his nerves and muscles! how easy his whole frame! . . . By these exercises the bodies of the Greeks got the great and manly Contour observed in their statues, without any bloated corpulency."[14] If West had not compared the *Apollo Belvedere* to a Mohawk warrior, Winckelmann could have done it for him. And since Galt's account of the comparison starts with Cardinal Alessandro Albani's mistaken belief that West himself was a savage,[15] and since in 1760 Winckelmann was in Rome employed as Cardinal Albani's librarian, he may indeed have supplied the idea. Be that as it may, if in mid-eighteenth-century minds the *Apollo* looked like an Indian, it follows that an Indian should look like the *Apollo*.

Shortly after his move to England, West provided two illustrations for a book by Provost Smith describing the expedition of a battalion of British soldiers into the Indian territory of Ohio in 1764 (see cat. 55). Drawn to accompany a text written by a member of a frontier society, West's Ohio Indians are savages who kidnap English children and must be chastened by white men. His earlier *Savage Warrior*, by contrast, is a model of domesticity. He is a husband and father of two children; has a dog, a home, and various household utensils; and grows corn, to which he points to assure his family that they will have sustenance as he departs to do his military duty. He is a noble savage in an arcadian and pastoral golden age far from cities and civilization: the natural man of Jean-Jacques Rousseau, whose ideas and

Cat. 6. *Angelica and Medoro*. (ca. 1763–1764)
Oil on canvas. 36¼ x 28¼ in. (92.1 x 71.8 cm.)
University Art Gallery, State University of New York
at Binghamton

those of Winckelmann were not unrelated. In leaving the new world, West chose civilization in preference to the simple life extolled by Rousseau, but Europe enabled him to visualize as ideal what previously, from closer to the actuality, must have seemed more like deprivation and hardship, and the freshly discovered dream of arcadia pervades his art of the 1760's. As the savage warrior and his squaw dwell harmoniously in the remote North American wilderness, so *Angelica and Medoro* of 1763–1764 (cat. 6) and *Venus and Adonis* of 1767 (see cat. 56) are happy denizens of the field and forest of European myth and literature.

Angelica and Medoro (cat. 6) illustrates *Orlando Furioso*, the epic poem by Ludovico Ariosto, published in final form in 1532. Angelica, a princess of Cathay, has nursed, fallen in love with, and married a beautiful Moorish youth, Medoro, whom she had found wounded in a forest near Paris. The painting shows them on their idyllic honeymoon in the woods, during which they carved their intertwined names on every rock and tree. Their right hands clasped, his foot caressed by hers, and watched over by cupids, Medoro points with his left hand to the name "Angelica" inscribed on the tree trunk before them. When West painted *Angelica and Medoro* he did have a friend named Angelica, the painter Angelica Kauffmann, whom he had met in Florence in 1762, and the subject was perhaps intended as a compliment to her. It is, or was, the companion to the *Cymon and Iphigenia* (now lost), which West painted before leaving Rome, and which also depicted a subject of bucolic romance. Both were shown, together with the portrait of *General Monckton* (cat. 7), at the Society of Artists in the spring of 1764 as the artist's first exhibited works in England. We do not know if West painted *Angelica and Medoro* in Rome, began it there and completed it in London, or painted it entirely in England, but, apart from *The Death of Socrates* of 1756 and the *Savage Warrior* done for ethnographic purposes, it is his earliest subject picture now known, and it demonstrates his progress after three years in Italy.

The intimate scale and theme of amorous escape into a pastoral never-never land, complete with a pair of lambs in the lower right corner, make *Angelica and Medoro* at least superficially reminiscent of countless confectionery scenes of dallying shepherds and shepherdesses by the French rococo artist François Boucher. If West painted *Angelica and Medoro* only after his arrival in London, he may indeed have been inspired by works by Boucher, such as *La Cage* of 1763 (Louvre), which he saw during his visit to Paris in the summer of 1763. Before then, in Italy, he had some exposure to contemporary French painting because of the French Academy in Rome, where Jean-Honoré Fragonard and Hubert Robert were students when he arrived. Its director was Charles Natoire, a contemporary and kindred spirit to Boucher. Nevertheless, our sources record no encounters between West and his French counterparts in Italy, whereas we are aware of his contacts with Anton Raphael Mengs,

Nathaniel Dance, Angelica Kauffmann, and the leading Italian painter working in Rome, Pompeo Batoni. Among the works of these artists, *Angelica and Medoro* is most similar in style, subject, and sentiment to those of Angelica Kauffmann, but she was three years younger than West, who influenced her more than she influenced him. The similarity reflects common concerns shared by the circle of artists around Batoni. Despite West's professed admiration for Mengs, *Angelica and Medoro* is more graceful, more sentimental, and less classicizing than Mengs's works of circa 1760–1761, and since Mengs left Rome for Spain in 1761, West did not see him after then. He would turn back to Mengs later as his art evolved in England.

The subject of *Angelica and Medoro* was popular in eighteenth-century Italy and there are numerous Italian renderings of it, such as the fresco by Tiepolo of 1757 in the Villa Valmarana near Vicenza, which West may have seen. Although there is no significant resemblance between his picture and Tiepolo's, or any other known painting of the subject, contemporary and near contemporary painting rather than the earlier masters he had been studying and copying, defined the ambitions underlying it. Yet West was not a Tiepolo or Boucher. He did not have the technical skills to foreshorten figures and link them in flowing baroque compositions comparable to theirs, nor any of their coloristic gifts. The relative simplicity and chastity of his *Angelica and Medoro*, epitomized by Angelica's strict profile, were dictated by what he could not do, as well as by what he chose to do. That they seem to point forward to the greater severity and chastity of his neoclassical paintings from the end of the 1760's is an early indication of his ability to make virtues out of his limitations.

In the years following 1764, his pictures became larger, more complex, and more allusive to the art he had seen in Italy. We can see this development in two compositions of related subjects: *Venus Relating to Adonis the Story of Hippomenes and Atalanta* (see cat. 56), which he exhibited at the Society of Artists in 1767, and *Venus Lamenting the Death of Adonis*, signed and dated 1768 (cat. 10), which he sent to the first exhibition of the new Royal Academy in 1769. The former is a reworking of the *Venus and Adonis* by Titian (which exists in many versions), with overtones of Correggio and of other works by Titian, including the *Venus of Urbino* which West had copied in Florence.[16] The latter was prefigured by a *Venus Lamenting the Death of Adonis* then ascribed to Annibale Carracci, which West also copied in Florence in 1762.[17] West's knowledge of Italian art was paraded not only in the subjects and compositions of these works, but also in technique. Charles Willson Peale, who arrived in London in February 1767 and saw the pictures West was about to exhibit, wrote back to America that they were "Painted in a Masterly Style and a Different Manner from Common Oil Painting, which gives great luster & strength to the Colouring—a method of Art no painter here

VENUS RELATING TO ADONIS, THE STORY OF HIPPOMENES AND ATALANTA.

Cat. 56. *Venus Relating to Adonis the Story of Hippomenes and Atalanta.* 1769
Engraving in reverse by John Hall
Sheet: 18 x 22¾ in. (457 x 578 mm.)
The Baltimore Museum of Art: Garrett Collection (BMA 1946.112.15443)

Else knows any thing of." West himself later declared that in the 1760's "His mind was full of Correggio."

The story of Venus and Adonis comes from Ovid's *Metamorphoses*. Venus, accidentally pricked by Cupid's arrow, has fallen in love with the beautiful youth Adonis. The earlier of West's two compositions shows the infatuated couple in their bucolic retreat, joined together like the two doves tied together with a string by a cupid on the right. But Adonis, holding his spear and accompanied by a hound, is a hunter, and the title under which West exhibited the painting in 1767 and which appears on the print reproducing it (cat. 56) refers to a tale which the goddess tells her lover as a warning to avoid savage beasts (in it Atalanta and Hippomenes are turned into lions). Naturally, Adonis disregards the advice and, while hunting, is killed by a wild boar. Venus in her grief turns him into the most fragile of wildflowers, the anemone. Cat. 10 shows Venus and Cupid bending over the dead Adonis, while flowers bloom behind him. Behind the flowers are the swans that pull Venus's chariot; on the left Adonis's hounds continue to pursue the boar. West evidently did not intend the two pictures as companions (they are of different sizes and were not exhibited together); nevertheless, the later painting is a narrative sequel that transforms our reading of the earlier scene from one of unalloyed contentment like *Angelica and Medoro* (who return to Cathay to live happily ever after) into an image full of premonition of what is to come.

Since in *The Death of Socrates* the hero is still very much alive, the treatment of death and of grief for the deceased in *Venus Lamenting the Death of Adonis* had no precedent in West's art except in copies, but it would soon be repeated in *The Death of General Wolfe* (cat. 13) painted two years later. The tragic content, paralleled by that of West's contemporaneous historical subjects discussed in the next chapter, signals the end of his rococo celebration of carefree love in the wild. After 1770 he would not abandon scenes of romantic love drawn from myth and literature, but such love is always seen as more complicated than it had been before. Romeo and Juliet, whom West painted around 1775 (cat. 20), are actors in a tragedy, not a pastoral romance, and his painting of them is about separation, sorrow, and the precariousness of happiness. Even in pictures in which

he returned to his subjects of the mid-1760's there are new messages.

Cat. 19 of 1773 shows *Cymon and Iphigenia*, the same subject that West had painted in Rome in 1763. It is based on a story in the *Decameron* as retold in English verse by John Dryden. Cymon, the doltish son of rich parents, is so backward that he has been sent to the country to live with the peasants. He comes upon Iphigenia asleep, and the sight of her beauty not only makes him fall in love, but shakes him out of his dull-witted state. Most pictures of the subject show the oafish Cymon looking at a sleeping and usually bare-breasted Iphigenia, but West's heroine, although accompanied by two sleeping companions, one of them bare-breasted, is herself wide awake and stylishly dressed. Another oddity is that the painting's provenance establishes that West sent it to the Royal Academy in 1776 under a patently incorrect title, as "Rinaldo and Armida," from *Gerusalemme liberata* by Torquata Tasso, whom he did depict correctly as described by Tasso in several other works.[18] The provenance also establishes that West painted the picture for the second Earl of Buckinghamshire, for whom he also painted a companion picture of an Old Testament subject, *Isaac's Servant Tying the Bracelet on Rebecca's Arm*.[19] Since both paintings depict the same elegant model as the object of the rapturous or respectful attention of a subordinate man, it seems probable that the earl commissioned the two as allegorical portraits of his second wife, whom he married in 1770, embodying his adulation of her. In a portrait, the sitter should be seen to best advantage, awake rather than asleep, and of course, not half-nude. And as her admirer would inevitably be equated with her husband—in the *Decameron* Cymon and Iphigenia get married—he should not be publicly catalogued as a half-witted oaf; hence the change of title transforming Cymon into Rinaldo, a crusader knight, who is enchanted and enraptured by a beautiful sorceress. Painted a decade after West's arrival in England, *Cymon and Iphigenia* demonstrates the flowering of his art; its technical advance upon *Angelica and Medoro* is manifest. Thematically, the imagery is no less idyllic, but the idyll is now at the service of worldly considerations that the artist could hardly have conceived ten years before.

Cat. 20. *Romeo and Juliet.* (ca. 1775)–1778
Oil on canvas. 44½ x 59 in. (113.1 x 150 cm.)
New Orleans Museum of Art:
Museum Purchase through Women's Volunteer Committee Funds

Cat. 9. *Robert Auriol Hay Drummond, 9th Earl of Kinnoull,
and His Brother, Thomas Drummond.* 1767
Oil on canvas. 94¾ x 58½ in. (240.8 x 148.6 cm.)
Addison Gallery of American Art, Phillips Academy,
Andover, Massachusetts

3. Wielding the Club of Hercules

In 1771 West wrote to his old friend John Green reporting on his situation and on the happy state of art in London, which under George III bid fair to vie with Paris and Rome:

> The Exhibitions hear have drove men to pursue defirent departments in the art of pinting—amongst which I have undertaken to whele the club of Herculus—in plain English I have imbarked in Historical painting—by which meanes I have removed that long received opinion that That was a department in the art that never would be incourage in the Kingdom. But I can say I have been so fare successfull in it that I find my pictures sell for a prise that no living artist ever received before.[1]

Annual exhibitions, which had only begun in England in 1760, did revolutionize English art, particularly after the establishment in 1768 of the Royal Academy. The opportunity to display their works to a growing public meant that artists could do more than satisfy patrons' demands for portraits by starting to create an art meant for the edification and enjoyment of large audiences rather than a single private purchaser. Nevertheless, somebody had to pay the bills. West's historical painting may have been intended as a public art that would make its impact in exhibitions, but his first important steps as a historical painter were taken at the behest of patrons, whose interests they embody as much or more than his own.

In 1768 he exhibited four paintings at the Society of Artists (the predecessor of the Royal Academy): one of a mythological subject: *Venus and Europa*;[2] one from the Old Testament: *Jacob Blessing the Sons of Joseph* (cat. 8); one from Roman history: *Agrippina Landing at Brundisium with the Ashes of Germanicus* (cat. 11); and one portrait (cat. 9). The latter two were painted for the same patron: Robert Hay Drummond, Archbishop of York and younger son of the ninth Earl of Kinnoull. The portrait shows Drummond's eldest sons: Robert and Thomas, sixteen and fifteen years old, as students wearing academic gowns. A globe and

books lie at their feet; a statue of Minerva, goddess of wisdom and learning looks over them; Robert points with his right hand to a temple, which is inscribed with the words *VIRTUTIS* and *HONORIS*; and in his left hand is a scroll, upon which the name *Regulus* is legible. Such details make the painting more than likenesses of two adolescent boys. It is an allegorical portrait, which recalls several paintings by Pompeo Batoni of the *Choice of Hercules* in which Virtue personified by Minerva points to a temple of honor on a distant hill.[3] The allegory speaks of education, ancient Rome, virtue, and honor, all of which were concerns of the boys' father, the Archbishop of York, about whom another son wrote, "his knowledge of history, ancient and modern, was most accurate, extensive and profound. It was the favorite topic of his familiar hours of instruction with his children; . . .[from it he deduced] the most useful remarks on government, manners, morals, and religion." The archbishop concerned himself not only with the instruction of his children, but also with that of West, repeating some of the roles performed by William Henry and Provost Smith in Pennsylvania. Galt tells us the manner in which he commissioned *Agrippina Landing at Brundisium with the Ashes of Germanicus*: during a conversation at dinner when West was a guest, the prelate addressed himself "with particular emphasis to his sons," sent one of them to the library for the relevant volume of Tacitus, and, having read the passage, he "commented on it at some length, in order to convey to Mr. West an idea of the manner in which he was desirous the subject should be treated."

The story told by Tacitus, radically abbreviated, is that Germanicus, the nephew and adopted heir of the Emperor Tiberius, died suddenly of a mysterious illness while on campaign in Syria. Since he was highly popular, it was immediately suspected that he had been poisoned at the instigation of Tiberius, who feared him as a potential rival. His widow, Agrippina, who had traveled with him, returned to Rome with his cremated remains, seeking justice, which

Cat. 11. *Agrippina Landing at Brundisium with the Ashes
of Germanicus.* 1768
Oil on canvas. 64½ x 94½ in. (164 x 240.1 cm.)
Yale University Art Gallery, Gift of Louis M. Rabinowitz

Cat. 12. *The Departure of Regulus from Rome.* 1769
Oil on canvas. 88½ x 120 in. (224.9 x 304.9 cm.)
Her Majesty Queen Elizabeth II

she never received although an inconclusive inquiry was held. The painting shows her at the moment of arrival back in Italy at the Adriatic port of Brundisium (the modern Brindisi), her son, the future Emperor Caligula, and her daughter Agrippina the younger, who would be the mother of Nero, on either side. As described by Tacitus, they were met by a crowd of mourners. "When Agrippina descended from the vessel with her two children, clasping the funeral urn, with eyes rivetted to the earth, there was one universal groan."

West's depiction of this scene of grief so pleased the archbishop that he arranged for the artist to show it to George III, who was sufficiently impressed to ask West to paint another Roman subject, *The Departure of Regulus from Rome* (cat. 12) for him. West completed it the year after *Agrippina* and at the explicit instruction of the king sent it, together with *Venus Lamenting the Death of Adonis* (cat. 10), to the first exhibition of the Royal Academy in 1769.

Marcus Atilius Regulus was a Roman consul and general in the third century B.C. In the first Punic War the Carthaginians took him prisoner, but promised his release if he negotiated peace or the return of Carthaginian prisoners in exchange for himself. Sent to Rome under the condition that he would return to Carthage if the proposals that he carried were not accepted, he nonetheless persuaded the Roman Senate to decline the terms as dishonorable and unfavorable to Rome. He then rejected all pleas from family, friends, and fellow citizens to remain in Rome, and, true to his word, returned to Carthage where he knew that torture and death awaited him. West's picture shows him about to depart after the Carthaginian emissaries, spurning the appeals of the friends who kneel around him, and turning his back on his wife, Marcia, who has fainted, and on their infant children. The ship that will carry him away is visible through the colonnade on the right.

According to Galt, George III, in emulation of Archbishop Drummond, himself read to West from Livy, where, in fact, there is only an abbreviated mention of Regulus. However, we know that West had heard of Regulus before that royal act, since Regulus's name appears on the portrait of the Drummond brothers, which is signed and dated 1767. Regulus's refusal to put himself or his family before the honorable discharge of his duty was celebrated by ancient writers, including Cicero and Horace, and by later students of history as the epitome of Roman republican virtue. His name on the portrait of Archbishop Drummond's sons is a talismanic sign of the Enlightenment belief in the study and emulation of such models of behavior, and it heralds the adulation of republican Rome and what it stood for among those thinkers who shaped the ideas underlying the American Revolution of 1776 and the French Revolution of 1789. The subordination of self and family to a higher duty extolled in *The Departure of Regulus from Rome* also anticipates Roman republican themes painted twenty years later by Jacques-Louis David on the eve of the French Revolution, notably *The Lictors Returning to Brutus the Bodies of His Sons* (1789; Louvre), which presents a similar message (David had initially proposed a painting of Regulus to fulfill the state commission that led to his *Brutus*). To some extent, West had anticipated such subjects in *The Death of Socrates* of 1756 (cat. 2), but his Socrates is essentially an object of sympathy. Even Agrippina of the year before is a victim, whose grief is the chief subject of the picture. But Regulus, pushing aside friends and family, acts resolutely and philosophically on principle. And there is no mistaking the meaning of his act. The story was familiar to every educated person in the eighteenth century, and pointing fingers, upraised arms, and despondent faces declaim it with rhetorical hyperbole. In comparison with *Angelica and Medoro* and related works from the preceding years, *Agrippina* and *Regulus* are not only larger, as befits public art—they were West's largest compositions to date—but more complex. Their protagonists are surrounded by multitudes of spectators and fellow actors, whose presence conveys the public meanings of their activities as emphatically as the bucolic isolation of Angelica and Medoro does the personal and private significance of theirs.

In the year that West exhibited his *Regulus* at the Royal Academy, one of the most-discussed French predecessors of David's pictures of the 1780's appeared in the Salon in Paris, *The Emperor Septimus Severus Reproaching His Son Caracalla for Having Plotted Against His Life* by Jean-Baptiste Greuze (Louvre). The coincidence demonstrates that West's adoption in the 1760's of subjects that we associate with a later moment in French art did have parallels in France. But, in contrast to West's success, the tepid contemporary response to Greuze's painting reflects, among other things, its less than compelling moral content (one should not try to assassinate one's father) and lack of narrative clarity. On the other hand, virtually any French painting has a grace and beauty of execution that make West's *Regulus* and *Agrippina* seem heavy-handed and even primitive simply as painting. Was that evident deficiency one more demonstration of technical limitations resulting from inadequate training, or was it deliberate?

An answer to that question must consider the nature of the paintings. Agrippina and Regulus were actual ancient Romans, whose landing and departing were (or purportedly were) recorded historical events; they were not mythical Olympian gods. West's paintings of them were not meant to please in poetic fashion, but to instruct in the manner of history. In this fundamental respect they differ from paintings of subjects from classical myth dedicated to allegorical and decorative ends. Like historical texts, West's reconstructions of ancient events were supposed to tell the truth, and for that an unvarnished, unembellished style was more serviceable than a more obviously artistic one. Additionally, the subjects of suffering, self-denial, and stern devotion to duty demand a formal sobriety in keeping with the sober lessons they impart. In selecting such subjects, West or his

Cat. 10. *Venus Lamenting the Death of Adonis.* 1768/1819
Oil on canvas. 62 x 68 in. (157.5 x 172.8 cm.)
The Carnegie Museum of Art, Pittsburgh: Purchase, 1911

patrons implicitly rejected the luxury and decadence of the ancien régime as firmly as the asceticism of the paintings rejected the stylistic equivalents. If West had been capable of painting with rococo grace, and if he had wanted to, he would not have painted better versions of these pictures. Whatever the means at his disposal, the means displayed in these works were appropriate to the ends. He may have painted certain kinds of pictures because he could not paint others, but he did so with conviction. The rational order, discipline, and dignity of his compositional structures are pictorial equivalents of the philosophical principles that the actions of Agrippina and Regulus embody.

When West showed *Agrippina Landing at Brundisium with the Ashes of Germanicus* to George III, he mentioned that it was surprising that the subject had not been painted by Poussin, "who was so well qualified to have done it justice, and to whose genius it was in so many respects so well adapted." Poussin had in fact painted a famous *Death of Germanicus* (Minneapolis Institute of Arts), to which West's work is a narrative sequel, and the example of Poussin was undoubtedly of importance to him. The compositions of the *Agrippina* and the *Regulus* are also full of echoes of the supreme examples of monumental public art in European painting: Raphael's frescoes in the Vatican. West had of course studied Raphael when he was in Rome, but Galt tells us that the frescoes had not initially interested him, and only after many visits could he appreciate the "fullness of their excellency."[4] Although he based a work (cat. 4) on Raphael's Madonnas as early as 1762, it was only after several years in England that his study of the frescoes, augmented by knowledge of Raphael's tapestry cartoons in the English royal collection, started to be an important factor in his art. In 1762 Anton Raphael Mengs ranked Raphael above Titian and Correggio as a model to emulate;[5] so in turning to Raphael, after a period of inspiration from Titian and Correggio, West was following advice he had almost certainly received in Rome. His *Agrippina* and *Regulus* might be thought of as the progeny of neoclassical pictures that he had seen there, among which the most celebrated was Mengs's *Parnassus* painted on the ceiling of the Villa Albani in 1760–1761, but West's works of 1768 and 1769 probably owed more to what he had digested from Mengs's instruction than to memory of his works, which they do not particularly resemble. Another artist in Rome while West was there, the Scot Gavin Hamilton, painted an *Agrippina Landing at Brundisium with the Ashes of Germanicus* (Tate Gallery) at roughly the same time as West, which, since the subject was not common, was probably not entirely coincidental; nevertheless, the differences between West's and Hamilton's paintings are greater than their similarities and demonstrate that West had created a convincing and consistent language of his own in the eight years since he had left America. What he and Hamilton primarily shared were a precocious admiration for Poussin and allegiance to the same type of moralizing historical subjects.

Despite the label "neoclassical" that is always attached to *Agrippina* and *Regulus* they do not show as much formal affinity with actual works of classical art as they do with sixteenth- and seventeenth-century paintings by Raphael and Poussin, for the obvious reason that classical antiquity did not provide comparable models of painting. In the *Savage Warrior* (cat. 54), West had demonstrated his acquaintance with the *Apollo Belvedere*, but in large compositions filled with masses of relatively small figures, what he had assimilated from classical sculpture could not be as significant as in pictures showing single figures or small groups of figures. Thus the strictly formal vocabulary of the contemporary but simpler *Venus Lamenting the Death of Adonis* is perhaps more classical than that of *Regulus*, and even the Old Testament *Jacob Blessing the Sons of Joseph* more singlemindedly displays the frieze-like grouping, sculptural clarity, and formal simplifications that we associate with the neoclassical style.

There are, nevertheless, two noteworthy borrowings from antique sources in *Agrippina*. The main group of Agrippina, her children, and her companion women recalls sculptural reliefs on the Roman *Ara Pacis Augustae*, which West had drawn while in Italy; and the portico and arcade in the center of the picture are taken from one of the first major monuments of archaeological publications, Robert Adam's *Ruins of the Palace of the Emperor Diocletian at Spalatro*, published in 1764. Archbishop Drummond, who commissioned West's painting and told him how he wanted it painted, was one of the original subscribers to Adam's book. These borrowings are central to the composition formally, but the specific sources have a relevance that is more than formal. The *Ara Pacis* reliefs were carved only a few years before the event depicted in the painting; the frieze shows the Imperial family in procession and includes as children both Germanicus and Agrippina, the granddaughter of the Emperor Augustus, thereby making them the models for their children as painted by West. Diocletian's palace was built almost three centuries later, but it was a Roman palace overlooking the Adriatic Sea, upon which the ancient port of Brundisium was also situated. West's building is adapted from Adam's reconstruction of the facade fronting the sea. Both sources were useful visual documents; aids in shaping as accurate a reconstruction of the event as the artist could muster. They were models of style as well, not because of their timeless classical beauty, but because they belonged to a time and were stylistically and historically appropriate to the subject.

What is at the core of *Regulus* and *Agrippina*, West's most important paintings of classical subjects, is not classical art per se, nor an attempt to recreate the noble simplicity and calm grandeur that Winckelmann found in works such as the *Apollo Belvedere*, but classical history and belief in the moral superiority of ancient Greece and Rome. For West, the compelling power of that belief lasted only a few years. After 1770 his most ambitious historical subjects would be

Cat. 18. *Chryses, the Priest of Apollo, on the Seashore, Invoking
His God to Avenge the Injuries Done Him by Agamemnon.* 1773
Oil on canvas. 50 x 40 in. (127.1 x 101.6 cm.)
Mount Holyoke College Art Museum,
South Hadley, Massachusetts:
The Warbeke Museum Fund, 1982

drawn from more recent times, while his paintings of classical subjects would be more modest in scale. The most successful of them turned back to the world of myth, allegory, and beauty. *Chryses, the Priest of Apollo, on the Seashore, Invoking His God to Avenge the Injuries Done Him by Agamemnon* of 1773 (cat. 18) illustrates the opening lines of the *Iliad*. The Greek leader Agamemnon has seized

Fig. 2. Thomas Watson (English, 1743–1781)
Alderman John Sawbridge. 1772
Mezzotint. 24⁵⁄₁₆ x 14⁷⁄₈ in. (618 x 378 mm.)
Photograph courtesy The British Museum

Chryseis, the daughter of Chryses, priest of Apollo in Chryse near Troy, and has spurned Chryses's pleas for her return. The old priest is seen walking along the shore, praying to Apollo to avenge Agamemnon's refusal, the gifts he has offered as ransom lying rejected at his feet. Apollo responds by inflicting a plague upon the Greeks, which forces Agamemnon to return Chryseis to her father. But Agamemnon takes Briseis from Achilles to fill her place,

and this act provokes Achilles's anger and withdrawal from the Trojan War, the major conflict in the first book of the *Iliad*, to which Chryses's troubles are only incidental background.

In 1760 Gavin Hamilton had commenced an immensely influential series of paintings based on the *Iliad*, which West knew both directly from Rome and indirectly from engravings after them. West himself had painted subjects from the *Iliad* prior to 1773, the first probably in 1766, which, although less ambitious, do not differ radically from *Agrippina* and *Regulus*, but his *Chryses* departs from both his and Hamilton's earlier depictions in significant ways. First, unlike all of those works, from which the gods are absolutely excluded, it shows Chryses praying for divine intervention and includes the god, Apollo, in his chariot in the sky. The presence of a deity who can decide human affairs calls into question the significance of human actions such as those held up as models of behavior in West's pictures of Agrippina and Regulus. Secondly, it shows an unusual subject rather than one of the familiar set pieces painted by Hamilton such as *The Anger of Achilles* or *The Parting of Hector and Andromache* (which was the subject of West's first *Iliad* painting of 1766, which has disappeared). The scene of a single figure in a setting of seacoast and sky is virtually unique among *Iliad* illustrations, and it places an emphasis upon nature and character, rather than, as more usually, upon the participants' actions. The priest with eyes turned to heaven is visibly the same old man that West had painted as *Simeon with the Child Jesus in His Arms* the year before (he also shows up in several other works painted between 1771 and 1774).[6] Both pictures affect us primarily as images of old age, for which the biblical and Homeric texts provide vehicles, and encourage suspicion that the visual source, the model, was more a factor in their conception than either literary source. In fact, the two paintings were part of a current vogue for picturesque old men. In the Royal Academy exhibition of 1772, Horace Walpole noted the features of one well-known model, "Old George" White, in no less than six different pictures. West painted White (of whom the best-known likeness is in Reynolds's *Ugolino* of 1773 at Knole House in Kent) several times,[7] but his *Simeon* of 1772 and *Chryses* of 1773 show another model, who remains unidentified.

In England and in the ambience of a Royal Academy led by Reynolds, the intrusion of an element of portraiture into paintings of classical subjects was perhaps inevitable, but classical subjects also crept into portraiture. Reynolds regularly exhibited pictures with titles such as *A portrait of a lady in the character of Juno, receiving the cestus from Venus* (1769), and West occasionally followed suit. The portrait of *Mr. and Mrs. John Custance* (cat. 26) shows a Norfolk squire (1749–1822) and his new wife, Frances Beauchamp-Proctor, the daughter of a neighboring squire, accompanied by Hymen, the Greek and Roman god of marriage. The painting appeared at the Royal Academy in 1779 as "A gentleman

Cat. 26. *Mr. and Mrs. John Custance*. 1778
Oil on canvas. 59 x 83 in. (150 x 210.9 cm.)
The Nelson-Atkins Museum of Art, Kansas City, Missouri
(Nelson Fund)

Cat. 19. *Cymon and Iphigenia.* 1773
Oil on canvas. 49 x 63 in. (124.5 x 160.1 cm.)
Los Angeles County Museum of Art:
Museum Purchase with Funds
Provided by Mr. and Mrs. Reese Llewellyn Milner,
Mr. and Mrs. Byron E. Vandergrift, George C. Zachary,
Jo Ann and Julian Ganz, Jr., and Joseph T. Mendelson

and lady in commemoration of their marriage." That event took place in 1778, and the classical details in the picture, which is signed and dated 1778, all allude to it. A cupid, torch in hand, tends the nuptial altar, and a second cupid lifts a veil to reveal the features of the bride. The groom, leaning on Hymen for support, takes her right hand in his left, while Hymen toys with his velvet toga. In the same year Mrs. Custance's brother also married, and West painted a portrait of his bride standing before the same altar and decorating a sculpted term of Hymen with flowers.[8] We have suggested that *Cymon and Iphigenia* (cat. 19) was an allegorical portrait of Lady Buckinghamshire as Iphigenia (and Armida), although it was not identified as such at the time. West did paint numerous explicitly allegorical portraits, of which the most memorable depicted a London alderman, John Sawbridge (1732–1795), as a Roman tribune (1772; destroyed, but known from an engraving, fig. 2). In that work, the subject was represented *as* someone else. His likeness in the garb of republican Rome became a manifesto not only of his devotion to Roman virtue, but also of his republican and anti-aristocratic political posture. Mr. and Mrs. Custance, on the other hand, are portrayed as themselves, clothed in a mixture of classical, contemporary, and seventeenth-century dress, and accompanied by allegorical figures and details pertaining to their marriage. The equal prominence of the living, breathing Hymen gives a startling equality to a part of the work that we would expect to be subordinate, as in West's *Lady Beauchamp-Proctor* or in pictures by Reynolds such as the well-known *Three Ladies Adorning a Term of Hymen* of 1774 (Tate Gallery). The nude figure was obviously inspired by classical sculpture: in particular it suggests a celebrated statue of Antinous (or Hermes), of which West had seen one version in the Vatican. More recently, another version had been excavated in 1771 (by Gavin Hamilton, who was an archaeologist and dealer as well as a painter) and exported to England;[9] so Hymen's large-as-life presence may have been prompted by sight of this work. Such an adaptation brings us almost full circle to the Winckelmannian admiration of the perfection of beauty of classical sculpture, to which West had been exposed in Rome. *Mr. and Mrs. John Custance* is a gracious record of an event of personal but no public significance. Apart from the likenesses of the two sitters, it presents nothing that we are expected to believe literally, and it uses classical detail in a playful manner to enrich its imagery visually as well as allegorically. In every respect it is the antithesis of the stern morality of *The Departure of Regulus from Rome*, which even treats the institution of marriage as something to be cast aside in the name of higher duty.

4. "A Revolution in the Art"

West probably began *The Death of General Wolfe* (cat. 13) shortly after completing *The Departure of Regulus from Rome* (cat. 12). Illness prevented him from finishing it in time to exhibit in 1770, but it is signed and dated 1770 and appeared at the Royal Academy in 1771. It shows Major-General James Wolfe, the commander of the victorious British forces, expiring from wounds he had received in the Battle of Quebec on September 13, 1759. Two of his officers point to a soldier carrying a captured French standard and running toward them with the news that the French were fleeing, news that elicited Wolfe's much-quoted last words, "Now, God be praised, I will die in peace." A distant figure falling from a horse on the hillside above the messenger probably represents Wolfe's adversary, the Marquis de Montcalm, who also died at Quebec. The St. Lawrence River is on the right, and scenes of artillery being dragged up the cliffs, troops mustering, and actual fighting unfold across the rest of the background. Six of the officers surrounding the dying general were identified in a key published in 1776. The most prominent of them, standing in the group to the left with his arm in a sling across his chest and supported by two other officers, is Brigadier-General Robert Monckton, the second in command at Quebec, who was wounded in the battle. The American Indian in the left foreground and the man behind him wearing moccasins and the green uniform of an American ranger are not identified in the key, but the powder horn carried by the latter is inscribed with the name of an American hero in the war against the French, General Sir William Johnson from upstate New York. The two soldiers standing on the right, who are also not identified in the key, were described in 1821 as "a Grenadier of the General's own regiment, and his servant, lamenting his fate."

The event took place ten years before West started to paint it. With the self-evident exception of Wolfe, the participants identified in the key were all alive in 1769. They wear contemporary uniform, and in this respect the picture appears radically unlike *Regulus*. While West was working on it, unsympathetic reports reached George III, who told the artist, "that it was thought very ridiculous to exhibit heroes in coats, breeches, and cock'd hats." According to Galt, Archbishop Drummond, fearing that West would damage the reputation he had achieved by the *Agrippina* and the *Regulus*, enlisted Reynolds to dissuade him from the risk. Reynolds argued "that the classic costume of antiquity" was more appropriate to the inherent greatness of the subject than "the modern garb of war," while West's chief claim in reply was: "the same truth that guides the pen of the historian should govern the pencil of the artist. I consider myself as undertaking to tell this great event to the eye of the world; but, if instead of the facts of the transaction, I represent classical fictions, how shall I be understood by posterity! . . . I want to mark the date, the place, and the parties engaged in the event." West persevered, and sight of the finished work forced Reynolds, as quoted by Galt, to eat humble pie: "I foresee that this picture will not only become one of the most popular, but occasion a revolution in the art."

The concern of the archbishop about West's reputation is easy to understand, and any hint that West might abandon his devotion to the high-minded subjects that academies were supposed to foster must have been frightening to the president of the Royal Academy. Reynolds's proposal of a more appropriate costume was in accord with his own efforts to ennoble portraiture by use of classical dress. Put into practice, it would have turned Wolfe and his men into Greeks and Romans, as the grandest paintings of modern subjects known to Reynolds and West, the allegorical series devoted by Rubens to Marie de Médicis now in the Louvre and the ceiling of the Galerie des Glaces at Versailles celebrating the victories of Louis XIV by Charles LeBrun, transformed their subjects. But West's concept of the role of the painter as equivalent to that of the historian, which already lay behind the *Agrippina* and *Regulus*, proscribed

Cat. 13. *The Death of General Wolfe.* 1770
Oil on canvas. 60 x 84 in. (152.5 x 213.4 cm.)
National Gallery of Canada, Ottawa:
Deposited by Canadian War Memorials Fund, 1921

allegory, although he did use it and put modern figures in classical costume in portraits such as that of Alderman Sawbridge (fig. 2).

Yet "the same truth that guides the pen of the historian" did not govern the painter of *The Death of General Wolfe*. The painting is almost as much a fiction as would have been one of soldiers in armor and togas. No American Indians served with the British at Quebec, and West's pensive warrior is, in effect, a symbolic noble savage, allegorically contemplating the alien intruders into his land, and anticipating in role as well as pose Rodin's *Thinker* brooding over the tortured souls in *The Gates of Hell*. Also, not one of Wolfe's named companions was with him at the time of his death; all were occupied with their own duties or suffering from their own wounds elsewhere on the field of battle. For some critics, their presence has made the painting no more than a pretentious conversation piece commemorating the visit of these English gentlemen to North America, and, in fact, West did paint two later replicas for the families of officers he had portrayed in it.[1] Nonetheless, he thought of the work as much more than portraiture and later defended the liberties he took as necessary to the "Epic representation" of the death of a hero:

> It must exhibit the event in a way to excite awe & veneration & that which may be required to give superior interest to the representation must be introduced, all that can shew the importance of the Hero. Wolfe must not die like a common soldier under a Bush . . . To move the mind there should be a spectacle presented to raise & warm the mind & all shd. be proportioned to the highest idea conceived of the Hero. . . . A mere matter of fact will never produce this effect.[2]

The "facts of the transaction" must be transformed and elevated above "mere matter of fact." Wolfe's fellow officers are there partly because West wanted to mark "the parties engaged in the event," partly, because their portraits enhance the illusion of verisimilitude and accuracy in the same manner as correct details of uniforms, and partly, because their presence gives Wolfe's death a public or epic dimension, just as the crowds of witnesses do for the actions of Agrippina and Regulus in his preceding pictures. That dimension is made resonant by the compositional similarity of the group around Wolfe to the mourners in Christian paintings of the lamentation over Christ's body after it has been lowered from the cross. Above Wolfe, the British Union Jack, across which gallops the white horse of Hanover, fills the place of the cross and provides a triumphant, if mournful, counterpart to the captured French fleur-de-lis linked with the falling Montcalm at the picture's left edge.

As Reynolds acknowledged, the subject had inherent greatness. The victory at Quebec was a significant triumph, not only assuring the security of the American colonies, but also by wresting Canada away from France, winning possession of what would become the world's second largest

country. In 1759 West had not yet left America, where the conflict had been close at hand. Four years previously General Edward Braddock's army had been annihilated at Fort Duquesne in western Pennsylvania. West's brother served with the troops that reoccupied Fort Duquesne, and the connection in West's mind between the campaigns in Pennsylvania and Canada is indicated by a proposal, which he made but never carried out, to paint a companion picture to *The Death of General Wolfe* showing the discovery of the bones of Braddock's army, known to him from Samuel West's witness account. By 1769 he had met British officers who had been at Quebec, chief among them General Monckton (cat. 7) and had gained a European perspective. His concept of epic representation transports a death in Canada in 1759 into the realm of the deaths of Patroclus and Hector (Gavin Hamilton's six *Iliad* paintings included both) or the death of Germanicus. The chief published account of the battle of Quebec, which appeared in 1769, not only referred to Wolfe as "this British Achilles," but in describing his dying words at the moment of victory added the following:

> This resignation, and greatness of soul calls to my remembrance an almost similar story of Epaminondas, the Theban general; who having received in a fight a mortal wound with a sword, which was left in his body, lay in that posture until he received intelligence that his troops had obtained victory, and then permitted it to be drawn out, saying, at that instant, "This is not the end of my life, my fellow-soldiers; it is now your Epaminondas was born, who dies in so much glory."

This parallel was also drawn by other commentators and is more than incidentally relevant to West's picture. When George III saw *The Death of General Wolfe*, like Reynolds he retracted his previous objections. He then commissioned West to paint a second version[3] and two companion pictures, one of which, proposed by West, was a *Death of Epaminondas* (see cat. 58; the other was cat. 16). This commission exemplifies the modern relevance that the late eighteenth century found in classical history. The equation of present and past explains to us the commitment of artists such as West to historical subjects. To their patrons it justified treating contemporary subjects with the same epic dignity as those from the classical past.

The mix of grand manner and contemporary factual reportage in *The Death of General Wolfe* had no precedent— or at least none that seems to have been of any importance to West—but it was an immense and immediate success, making the painting one of the best-known and most influential works of the eighteenth century. It did occasion a "revolution in the art," not only in England and America, but on the continent of Europe as well. It was echoed directly in a French *Mort du Marquis de Montcalm* painted by Watteau de Lille, in which reversing the tiny Montcalm in West's background, there is a distant tableau of the death

Cat. 16. *The Death of the Chevalier Bayard.* 1772
Oil on canvas. 87¼ x 70½ in. (221.7 x 179.1 cm.)
Her Majesty Queen Elizabeth II

Cat. 27. *The Death of the Earl of Chatham.* (ca. 1778/1786)
Oil on canvas. 28 x 35¾ in. (71.1 x 90.8 cm.)
Kimbell Art Museum, Fort Worth, Texas

of Wolfe quoted from West.[4] Subsequent beneficiaries of the revolution included the paintings of the martyrs of the French Revolution by David, whose progression from classical to modern history followed a trajectory parallel to West's and paintings of the Napoleonic wars by Baron Gros in France and Goya in Spain. West's own next efforts to paint sequels showing contemporary subjects in a comparably heroic fashion were, however, to prove abortive.

On April 7, 1778, William Pitt the Elder, who had been raised to the peerage as the first Earl of Chatham, collapsed in the House of Lords while speaking in a debate over the American war. He never recovered and died a few weeks later. West began a sketch of the event soon after, certainly within a year (cat. 27), but never carried it out as a large painting in order not to compete with John Singleton Copley, who by May 1779 had begun his own version of the subject (Tate Gallery).

The dramatically public end to Pitt's career, if not as Homeric as that of Wolfe, was rich in historic reverberations. The elder Pitt led the English government from 1757 to 1761 and was universally credited for Britain's success in the Seven Years' War. He held a special place in American hearts both because of the victories that had occurred under his aegis (the site of Braddock's defeat became Fort Pitt, or Pittsburgh, when retaken in 1758), and because of his subsequent defense of American liberties. That role is celebrated in a portrait painted in 1768 by West's pupil Charles Willson Peale of "the Great Commoner" as a Roman Consul (versions in the Westmoreland County Court House, Virginia, and in the Maryland State House, Annapolis), which anticipated West's *Alderman Sawbridge* as a Roman tribune (fig. 2), but was itself undertaken as the companion to an unrealized portrait previously commissioned from West to commemorate Lord Camden's opposition to the Stamp Act. Its allegorical content also echoes that of the *Drummond Brothers* of 1767 (cat. 9). By contrast, there is nothing allegorical about West's *Death of the Earl of Chatham*. The setting is the House of Lords as it looked until the fire of 1834, and the participants are members of the peerage who had been present on the fateful day. The "facts of the transaction" appear to speak for themselves.

Copley, on the other hand, in the large picture that he completed and exhibited in 1781 took greater liberties. According to Horace Walpole:

> Mr. West made a small Sketch of the death of Lord Chatham, much better expressed & disposed than Copley's. It has none but the principal person's present; Copley's almost the whole peerage, of whom seldom so many are there at once, & in Copleys most are meer spectators. but the great merit of West is the principal Figure which has his crutch & gouty stockings, which express his feebleness & account for his death. West wd not finish it not to interfere with his friend Copley.

In later years, West and Copley became bitter rivals, but West initially looked benevolently upon his compatriot's

reestablishment in London after fleeing Boston on the eve of the American Revolution. Upon settling in England Copley immediately began to paint modern subjects, of which his *The Death of the Earl of Chatham* was the second, following the more radical but less publicly oriented *Watson and the Shark* exhibited in 1778 (National Gallery of Art, Washington, D.C.). Its composition is enough like West's for us to infer either that they were developed jointly or that one was derived from the other. It would have been mutually destructive for such related works to compete with one another for public attention, but there was another dimension to the potential conflict. Traditionally, classical subjects, like religious ones, had been the common property of all artists, with the distinctive quality of the individual work determined not by choice of subject, but by the imagination and skill of the artist in carrying it out. "The Departure of Regulus" and "The Death of Epaminondas," for example, had been set as subjects of a competition sponsored by the Society of Arts in 1759. Contemporary historical events introduced a journalistic dimension of reporting the news and, hence, the importance of primacy in treating a potentially popular subject. In addition to the financial rewards to be earned by the first painting and the first engraving after it to reach the market, there was also a question, implied in Walpole's criticism of Copley, of how much variation in treatment there could be in different works purporting to record the same contemporary event in a factually convincing manner.

An ongoing contemporary event that promised to yield numerous sequels to *The Death of General Wolfe* of particular concern to an American-born artist was the American revolutionary war, to which in the summer of 1783 West wrote to Charles Willson Peale that he planned to devote a series of pictures. Cat. 30, which he began 1783, evidently as the first work in the series, shows the American participants in the preliminary peace conference between Britain and America in Paris in November 1782. They are, from left to right: John Jay, John Adams, Benjamin Franklin, Henry Laurens, and William Temple Franklin, Benjamin's grandson, who served as the Americans' secretary. On the unfinished right side would have been the British representative, Richard Oswald, and his secretary, Caleb Whiteford. According to John Quincy Adams, who accompanied his father when he sat to West in 1783, and who saw the canvas again in 1817, Richard Oswald was so ugly that he never allowed his portrait to be painted, thus making it impossible for West to include his likeness or complete the picture. It remains an unfinished sketch, the same size as *The Death of the Earl of Chatham*, rather than a history painting on public scale, which John Quincy Adams believed West intended to present when finished to the American Congress.

Four of the Americans posed for West in 1783 and 1784. The fifth, Benjamin Franklin, was an old acquaintance and godfather of West's second son, Benjamin, born in 1772 while Franklin was living in London as agent for Pennsyl-

Cat. 30. *American Commissioners of the Preliminary Peace
Negotiations with Great Britain.* (ca. 1783)
Oil on canvas. 28½ x 36½ in. (72.5 x 92.5 cm.)
Courtesy of the Henry Francis du Pont Winterthur Museum,
Winterthur, Delaware

vania. He did not return to London after the revolution, and West never painted him from life, but based his image in cat. 30 on copies of a portrait painted in 1778 by the French artist Joseph Siffred Duplessis. West was probably drawn to this particular scene by the opportunity to paint two American ambassadors, Jay and Adams, when they arrived in London in October 1783 (Laurens and William Temple Franklin had lived there on and off and were more regularly available), just as he was kept from finishing it by lack of opportunity to paint their British opposite number. The picture is primarily a commemorative group portrait and no narrative action indicates that the participants are doing anything more than posing for their portraits. Despite the importance of the treaty they were together to negotiate, the moment is perpetuated as a conversation piece showing five Americans abroad, in this respect recalling *The Cricketers* of 1763 (cat. 5) showing five other Americans abroad. The Place de la Concorde in Paris has replaced Cambridge in the background, and twenty years and a war lie between the two, but they show sitters from the same stratum of American society. The paths of three of the students shown in cat. 5 and four of their now older compatriots in cat. 30 did cross in the Continental Congress, where they variously served in the interval.

West carried his American revolutionary series no further. The frustration of being unable to complete the picture of the peace conference may have led him to foresee insurmountable difficulties in trying to paint convincing pictures of events in North America, whose participants were even less likely to be available to pose. Also, in the 1780's, when he had as much work as he could manage from George III, it seems unlikely that he could have found the time to carry out yet another ambitious project. But, most significantly and obviously, he must have realized that, as a courtier and Historical Painter to the King, he could not very well paint a series of works lauding American victory and English defeat. The series—or a series—was painted instead by one of West's pupils, John Trumbull, who commenced it in West's studio in 1785. Unlike West, Trumbull, who would return to pursue his career in America, had nothing to lose and everything to gain by the venture. He began by painting a variation on the imagery of *The Death of General Wolfe*, modified and updated to become *The Death of General Warren at the Battle of Bunker's Hill, 17 June 1775* (Yale University Art Gallery), and concluded some forty years later by winning a commission from Congress to paint large versions of four pictures from the series for the Rotunda of the United States Capitol. There they remain, dim products of Trumbull's declining later years, but the ultimate realization, never so completely attained by West himself, of what history painting was supposed to be: public art in a public place, serving a public purpose.

If West surrendered the field of contemporary history to Copley and Trumbull, he did follow his initial break from the histories of Greece and Rome with depictions of other periods, most notably the seventeenth century. The first was *Penn's Treaty with the Indians* (cat. 15), which is signed and dated 1771 and appeared at the Royal Academy in 1772. The encounter it shows supposedly had taken place ninety years previously, in 1682, when Penn concluded a treaty of peace with the local Lenape Indians shortly after his arrival in America. No actual treaty is known, and scholars tend to dismiss the event as apocryphal legend. Nevertheless, West believed that it had happened and claimed that his fellow Pennsylvanians venerated the spot where it occurred, now part of Philadelphia. The legend also had wider currency because it was seen to have more than local significance. In 1733, Voltaire praised Quaker pacificism by citing the agreement as the only treaty between Christians and native Americans that was never broken. West wrote in 1805: "The great object I had in forming that composition was to express savages brought into harmony and peace by justice and benevolence, by not withholding from them what was their reight, and giving to them what they were in want of, as well as a wish to give by that art a conquest made over native people without sward or Dagder."

The full title under which the picture was first exhibited was "William Penn's treaty with the Indians, when he founded the province of Pennsylvania in North America." What it depicts, along the shore of the Delaware, is a barter of goods for land. Penn points to a map held by one of his associates, while two others proffer a bolt of cloth, with more presumably to follow from the open trunk before them. In the right foreground a squaw nursing her papoose and accompanied by other children embodies the simple natural life that West had earlier represented in the *Savage Warrior* painted in Italy (see cat. 54), but that will soon be displaced by the busy activity of unloading ships and building houses going on in the background. The subject is not simply the treaty but the happy and harmonious colonization of Pennsylvania. West painted the picture for Thomas Penn, the son of William Penn and hereditary proprietor of the colony, and it has been argued that the peaceful scene carried a propagandistic message in support of the Penn family at a time when its role was under attack from many Pennsylvanians, including Benjamin Franklin.[5] The Reverend William Smith, West's old teacher in Philadelphia, was outspokenly Franklin's adversary and Penn's advocate, who even went briefly to jail in 1758 because of his loyalities. Chief Justice William Allen and Lieutenant-Governor James Hamilton, West's patrons, were also staunch members of the proprietary party—in 1766 Anne Allen, the chief justice's daughter whose portrait West painted,[6] married a nephew of Thomas Penn—so respect for the institutions Penn is seen establishing did have deep roots in West's milieu. Such subjects from the recent past, separated by only a generation or two from the artist himself, had the potential of bearing meanings of local and topical relevance more readily than ones from classical antiquity. When painted at the behest of individual patrons, as West's were, they easily could present

Cat. 15. *Penn's Treaty with the Indians.* 1771–(1772)
Oil on canvas. 75½ x 107¾ in. (191.8 x 273.8 cm.)
Pennsylvania Academy of the Fine Arts, Philadelphia:
Gift of Mrs. Sarah Harrison (The Joseph Harrison, Jr. Collection)

Cat. 21. *The Battle of La Hogue.* (ca. 1775–1780)
Oil on canvas. 60⅛ x 84⅜ in. (152.8 x 214.4 cm.)
National Gallery of Art, Washington, D.C.:
Andrew W. Mellon Fund 1959.8.1

the patron's point of view. However, West's images do not say anything that would have been found exceptionable by the public at the time; they embody generally shared values far more than pointed propagandistic messages. In the late twentieth century, we may interpret *Penn's Treaty* as a land grab and European exploitation of indigenous people, disguised under a cloak of benevolence and mutual respect, but it is unlikely that anyone in the eighteenth century, even Benjamin Franklin, would have seen it as other then a scene of virtuous behavior as honorable as that of the ancient Romans. That parallel is enhanced by West's formal language, which, despite details of beads, feathers, and three-cornered hats, is essentially the same as that of his *Agrippina* and *Regulus*, and gives to the event some of the same classic dignity.

Penn's Treaty was not undertaken as a companion to *The Death of General Wolfe*; it is, among other things, considerably larger. Nevertheless, painted a year later, it is West's only other major painting of a subject set in America, and Thomas Penn must have been inspired to want it by the success of its predecessor. In 1773 the print dealer John Boydell linked the two paintings in announcing the engravings after them which he had commissioned. The engraving after *The Death of General Wolfe* by William Woollett (cat. 61), which appeared on January 1, 1776, was the most popularly successful print of the eighteenth century and made a fortune for Boydell. The print of *Penn's Treaty* by John Hall was almost equally successful (cat. 59). Both demonstrate how felicitously West's compositions could be translated into the black-and-white medium of engraving, the absence of color indeed enhancing the gravity of the noble deeds and sacrifices shown. Moderately priced and produced in large numbers, the prints became more widely known than the paintings themselves. *General Wolfe* and *Penn's Treaty* eventually and appropriately came to public collections in Canada and the United States, but the engravings after them made both into familiar historical icons before they left the possession of the descendants of their original purchasers.

When George III's misgivings about "breeches and cock'd hats" kept him from purchasing the first version of *The Death of General Wolfe*, it was bought by a rich peer, Richard, Lord Grosvenor, who subsequently purchased (and presumably commissioned) four further pictures the same size depicting English subjects from the seventeenth century. The most admired of these was *The Battle of La Hogue* (cat. 21), which appeared at the Royal Academy in 1780, but may have been begun some years previously. It shows a naval victory of 1692 over the French, in which a detachment of British sailors under Admiral George Rooke managed, by using small boats, to slip through the enemy defenses and set fire to a dozen French warships in the Bay of La Hogue, near Cherbourg. The ships had been mustered in the Channel as part of a flotilla intended to carry a mixed French and Irish army to England in an attempt by Louis XIV to restore James II to the throne from which he had

been deposed by the Glorious Revolution of 1688.

Unlike *The Death of General Wolfe*, which treats the aftermath of victory as a static *tableau vivant*, *The Battle of La Hogue* shows the conflict itself and is full of excited and dramatic action. It has no single central focus but many separate incidents enacted by relatively small figures linked together by common participation in the struggle. The attacking English sailors surge across the canvas from left to right, while smoke from the burning French ships rises in the same direction. The action is communicated by boldly brushed and richly impasted paint, in place of the carefully drawn contours, thin handling, and finished surfaces of *The Death of General Wolfe* and West's earlier paintings of classical subjects. In effect, *The Battle of La Hogue* is a baroque battle scene, recalling Rubens more than Raphael and Poussin. Its radical alteration in style demonstrates West's flexibility in adapting his formal vocabulary to suit the demands of his subjects. It also foretells the richer and broader neobaroque manner that would characterize much of his painting of the 1780's in which we can generally discern the same linkage between content and form.

There is no single hero in the picture. Admiral Rooke, standing sword in hand in a small boat to the left of center, is no more prominent than the anonymous gun- and sword-wielding sailors under his command. Since no individual decision or act will determine the outcome of the conflict, no individual is as clearly delineated or characterized as a Regulus or a Wolfe; all are subordinated to a larger whole. Although the painting shows examples of humanity—at the center English sailors are saving their French foes from drowning—and bravery, it is above all a stirring scene of English victory and French defeat, not of martyrdom and self-sacrifice for the sake of high philosophical principles. The most vivid detail is on the right edge of the canvas, where a foppish and frightened Frenchman, who has lost his hat and wig, clings to a mast and tries ineffectually to save himself from his resolute opponents. On a cliff in the background above are discernible the small figures of James II and his courtiers, who were on hand to be carried triumphantly back to England. As the exiled monarch watched his hopes of resuming his throne destroyed, he is reported to have said, "None but my brave English tars could have performed so gallant an action." If West, exiled from his country, painted *The Battle of La Hogue* after France entered the revolutionary war on the American side early in 1778, its patriotic anti-French imagery would have been of timely if, as from the perspective of James II, bittersweet relevance.

General Monk Receiving Charles II on the Beaches of Dover (cat. 29) was also painted for Lord Grosvenor. Dated 1782 and exhibited in 1783, it shows the successful return to England in 1660 of James II's older brother, Charles II, following the death of Oliver Cromwell and the collapse of the Protectorate. While General Monk kneels before Charles, the future James II stands behind the brother he had

Cat. 29. *General Monk Receiving Charles II*
on the Beaches of Dover. 1782
Oil on canvas. 60 x 85 in. (152.5 x 216 cm.)
Layton Art Collection, Milwaukee Art Museum

accompanied in an earlier exile, along with a third brother, the Duke of Gloucester. The white cliffs of Dover in the background are on the opposite side of the Channel from the French cliffs overlooking La Hogue, on which James subsequently would stand. Since *La Hogue* and *General Monk* belonged to a series of four pictures illustrating episodes from a span of less than forty years of British history—the other two were *Oliver Cromwell Dissolving the Long Parliament* and *The Battle of the Boyne*[7]—the thematic counterpoint between them was more than coincidental. Yet timely considerations rather than a thought-out program for the series as a whole may have dictated the subject of the later work. West painted this scene of reconciliation ending a period of revolutionary strife after the British surrender at Yorktown, while negotiations to terminate the revolutionary war were under way. He began his painting of the American peace representatives (cat. 30) in the following year.

Compared to the excitement and action of *The Battle of La Hogue*, the ceremonious return of Charles II seems like a reversion to an earlier, more sober mode. The handling of paint is denser, the coloring is richer, and the groupings of figures are more complex than in West's paintings of the late 1760's and early 1770's, but the carefully balanced composition focusing on two central actors, each delineated in exact profile, has a consciously old-fashioned formality. Historically, however, the two main individuals were the ones that mattered. Unlike the tars in *The Battle of La Hogue*, the others are only spectators, who, as in earlier pictures, underline the public nature of the event. General George Monk, who engineered the return of Charles II, had inherited the power of Cromwell, but had not attempted to keep it. Depicted kneeling before the king in a salutary act of self-denial, he is an English equivalent of those ancients whose virtuous deeds provided the motivating content of much neoclassical history painting. But Charles II, who rewarded Monk by making him Duke of Albemarle, is the central actor. Monk's obeisance to his monarch, against whom he had previously fought, may have been intended to say something about reconciliation on behalf of Lord Grosvenor, who had had his difficulties with the royal family following his wife's well-publicized seduction by George III's younger brother, the Duke of Cumberland. Reconciliation was achieved and rewarded by his being elevated to an earldom in 1784. The manifestation of reverence toward the monarch spoke also, if only incidentally, for West who, before all else, was in the 1780's a servant of the crown.

Cat. 22. *St. Michael and Satan.* 1776
Oil on paper mounted on canvas. 45 x 28½ in. (114.3 x 72.4 cm.)
Collection of James Ricau on extended loan
to The Brooklyn Museum

5. A Pennsylvania Yankee at King George's Court

From 1768 to 1801 the presiding fact of West's career was his position at court. It gave him wealth, opportunities granted to no other artist, and power; his election as president of the Royal Academy in 1792 was due to his connection with the king. He described George III as "the best friend I ever had in my life." The two men shared years both of birth and death. In 1760 the king came to the throne, West arrived in Europe, and annual exhibitions commenced in England, leading to the creation of the Royal Academy in 1768. As patron of the body that he referred to as "my Academy," George III believed his royal duties to include support of the distinguished national school of painting that the Academy would engender; hence his patronage of West, who promised to be the bright star of such a school. In the words of John Galt:

> For the fine arts he had not, perhaps, any natural taste; . . .he was fully aware of the lustre which the arts have, in all ages, reflected on the different countries in which the cultivation of them has been encouraged to perpetuate the memory of great events. His employment of Mr. West, although altogether in his private capacity, was therefore not wholly without a view to the public advantage, and it is the more deserving of applause, as it was rather the result of principle than of personal predilection.[1]

It was no accident that *The Departure of Regulus from Rome*, West's most ambitious picture to date, which appeared in the first exhibition of the Royal Academy, was painted at the behest of the king. Writing to John Green in 1771, West had every reason to describe the arts in England as enjoying a new Augustan age under George III. But since he succeeded in attracting to himself all the royal largesse intended to support a native school of history painting, none of his colleagues would have seen the situation in quite so rosy a light.

George III signaled his approval of *The Departure of Regulus from Rome* by commissioning six further works to hang with it. The seven pictures, painted between 1768 and 1773, were installed in the Warm Room on the ground floor at the center of the garden facade of Buckingham House (now Palace), which was being remodeled by Sir William Chambers to serve as the London home of the royal family, and to which much of the royal collection was moved at this time.[2] In 1774 John Green came to London and was taken by West to Buckingham House. He reported that an apartment had been set apart for West's pictures, "and he has already filled it with storys from the Grecian, Latin, German, French, and English Historys, he told me that His Majesty chose the subjects."[3]

Although Green's report only accounts for five of the seven pictures in the Warm Room, it indicates that the otherwise puzzling diversity of their subjects was the organizing principle of a program dictated by the king. Opposite *The Departure of Regulus from Rome* hung an equally large *Oath of Hannibal*,[4] illustrating the opposing Carthaginian side in the Punic Wars. Two smaller overdoors showed the Persian emperor Cyrus and an obscure incident from Germanicus's campaigns in Germany, chosen because it showed the royal family's purported German ancestors.[5] The repetition of *The Death of General Wolfe* which West painted for the king added English history, and paintings commissioned to go on either side of it were chosen to represent other periods: *The Death of Epaminondas* "as a classic subject, and with Grecian circumstances," and *The Death of the Chevalier Bayard* (cat. 16), "which would serve to illustrate the heroism and peculiarities of the middle ages." [For Epaminondas, see cat. 58 and p. 112.] His opposite number, Pierre Terrail, Seigneur de Bayard (1473–1524), "*chevalier sans peur et sans reproche*" and the embodiment of French chivalry, had been the subject of eulogistic biographies published in France in 1760 and 1769, and a painting of one of his deeds by the English artist Edward Penny had appeared along with West's *Agrippina* at the Society of Artists in 1768. Bayard's death occurred in 1524 in Lombardy, where the French were fighting the armies of the emperor Charles V. Mortally wounded, he refused to be taken away by the retreating French, and was left alone to await the enemy. He is shown receiving their homage and calmly reciting the Miserere, while holding the hilt of his sword in the position of a cross.

The "peculiarities of the middle ages," displayed in armor, weapons, heraldry, costume, and a castle on a background hill, belonged to a different world than the ancient Rome of a Regulus and required not only different historical details, but also a style appropriate to the period and place shown. Although this "medieval" event occurred in Italy four years after the death of Raphael, West's visualization was shaped primarily by seventeenth-century painting, particularly that of van Dyck, whose armor-clad cavaliers from the beleaguered court of Charles I probably seemed to West to belong to the same vanished world of chivalry as Bayard from the century before. There are recognizable quotations, such as the horses' heads on the left and right bowed in equine homage to Bayard, which echo the horse in van Dyck's well-known portrait of Charles I in the Louvre, but more significant and equally redolent of van Dyck are the sense of movement and atmosphere, which has no precedent in West's earlier work, and the sunset colors in the sky that seem to convey nature's lament over the impending death.

When the walls of the Warm Room were filled in 1773, George III evidently had no place to put additional paintings, and the commissions abruptly stopped. In 1776 he put his Historical Painter to work painting portraits, but at the end of the decade new walls to cover and new opportunities for history painting on a far grander scale came into sight. This was due to a project begun in 1778 of restoring the great medieval castle at Windsor as a royal residence. Apart from portraits, which West continued to paint until 1783, all his work for George III after 1780 was done for Windsor. He took a house there, was given space in the castle in which to work, and starting in 1780 received an annual stipend of £1,000 from the crown.

The only strictly historical pictures that West painted for Windsor were seven subjects from the reign of King Edward III in the fourteenth century, commissioned for the king's Audience Chamber and painted between 1786 and 1789. *Edward III Crossing the Somme* belongs to the series, and *Edward the Black Prince, Receiving John, King of France, Prisoner, after the Battle of Poitiers* is a small version of one of three huge paintings, each approximately fifteen feet across.[6] In scale and as a group of thematically connected works, the paintings for the Audience Chamber constituted West's most monumental undertaking as a painter of historical subjects, the most ambitious group of pictures of medieval subjects produced by any artist in the eighteenth century, and an early landmark in the development of a tradition of painting subjects from English history or indeed from the national history of any country. All the episodes shown appear to have been drawn from David Hume's

History of England published between 1754 and 1762, but West also employed an impressive variety of other historical and antiquarian sources, including the contemporary fourteenth-century French *Chronicles* of Jean Froissart. The series may have been partly prompted by Bishop Richard Hurd, the preceptor to the Prince of Wales and Duke of York and author of a *Letters on Chivalry and Romance* published in 1762, but Galt and other sources emphasize that West himself did most of the requisite research:

> The historical pictures for Windsor Castle cost him many a patient hour of midnight research; for the means to assist his composition, especially in architecture, and the costume of the time, were then far from being so easy of access as they are at present. A long period of preference for classic literature, and the illustration of the Greek and Roman story, had withdrawn the public taste from the no less glorious events of our own annals.[7]

As in his paintings of modern history, West included portraits of the participants but since neither the people involved nor their likenesses were available, this portraiture consisted of identification via heraldic insignia on banners, shields, and elaborate crests on the helmets. For the king he provided long lists of the persons shown, accompanied by descriptions of their distinguishing insignia.

There were two explicit and connected reasons for devoting the series to Edward III. First, Windsor Castle, for which the paintings were intended, had been substantially given the form it still has during his reign. Second, Edward had founded the Order of the Garter, making St. George's Chapel at Windsor its spiritual home. One large picture in the series depicts the original institution of the Order of the Garter, and reinvigoration of the Order was a concern of George III. Like the refurbishment of Windsor Castle itself, that interest reflects the larger rediscovery of the middle ages in the later eighteenth century and the concomitant beginning of the Gothic revival in architecture and design. The glorification of medieval chivalry had been prefigured in *The Death of the Chevalier Bayard* of 1772, but with a difference in nationality. Whereas in Buckingham House patron and artist had gone out of their way to be international in their perspective, at Windsor the glory and the virtue were strictly English. Edward III had conducted brilliant military campaigns in France, and celebration of his victories over England's traditional foe constituted no small part of the room's message.

Cat. 32 shows an episode from an English sortie into northern France in the summer of 1346. With his small army about to be surrounded by a much larger French force, Edward found all the bridges over the river Somme either destroyed or heavily defended, closing his route of retreat. A peasant led him to a ford, into which the king bravely plunged at the head of his troops with the words, "Let those that love me, follow," and succeeded in crossing. Shortly after this escape, Edward gained his greatest victory

Cat. 32. *Edward III Crossing the Somme.* 1788
Oil on canvas. 54 x 59 in. (137.2 x 149.9 cm.)
Her Majesty Queen Elizabeth II
Copyright reserved to Her Majesty Queen Elizabeth II

Cat. 33. *Edward the Black Prince, Receiving John, King of France, Prisoner, after the Battle of Poitiers.* (ca. 1788)
Oil on canvas. 16½ x 25½ in. (41.9 x 64.8 cm.)
Collection George E. Doty, New York

at Crécy, a few miles to the north. Cat. 33 records a later victory, won at Poitiers in southwestern France in 1356 by Edward's son, the Prince of Wales, popularly known as the Black Prince. In this contest, the prince not only defeated an enemy army five times larger than his own, but even succeeded in capturing the French king and his son, the Dauphin. The large painting hung pendant to one the same size showing the conclusion of the battle of Crécy,[8] in which Edward III and his then fifteen-year-old son stand over the fallen king of Bohemia, whose coronet decorated with three ostrich feathers was to be adopted by the Prince of Wales. In cat. 33, wearing the ostrich feathers, the Black Prince receives his royal prisoners with courtesy, sympathy, and respect. Hume described this chivalrous behavior as the prince's real and truly admirable heroism, to which, in comparison, victories are vulgar things.

Bravery, as displayed by the king at the Somme, and chivalry, as by his son at Poitiers, are virtues, comparable to the principled self-sacrifice of a Regulus. But in these pictures, virtue is the property of hereditary princes, the forebears of West's patron, George III, and of his son, another Prince of Wales. Their companions, identified by their heraldic devices, are knights and lords, themselves forebears of aristocratic possessors in the eighteenth century of the same coats of arms as well as inherited rank, properties, privileges, and power. In the aftermath of the establishment of an egalitarian democracy in Britain's former American colonies, and on the eve of revolution in France, these glorifications of the ancestors of the present king and aristocracy echoed and reinforced assumptions about who and what mattered in history and society that many people had started to question. A contemporary review of the large *Battle of Poitiers* criticized the neatness and cleanness of the armor and clothing at the end of a hard-fought battle. The criticism is valid, but misses the point of the picture, which never was supposed to present a realistic depiction of a battle. It shows a meeting of princes, unsullied by the dirt and mess of actual warfare, but cosseted by all the picturesque heraldry and panoply of a noble entourage. Precisely that sort of meeting, perpetuating institutions and traditions born in the middle ages, is what was supposed to take place in the room in which the picture was intended to hang.

Although the pictures for the Audience Chamber seem to have been George III's favorites among West's works, engaging his interest "until he actually acquired a feeling like enthusiasm for the arts,"[9] they were overshadowed by a much larger scheme, which had been commenced earlier, to decorate the royal chapel in Windsor Castle.[10] Shortly after the formation of the Royal Academy, several of its members, including West, had proposed to decorate St. Paul's Cathedral in London with paintings, but the project was immediately vetoed by the bishop of London on the grounds of popery. West subsequently did win commissions from other prelates who did not share the bishop's views— *St. Michael and Satan* is a sketch for the altarpiece in the chapel of Trinity College in Cambridge completed in 1777, and cat. 64 is an engraving by Francesco Bartolozzi (who came to England the year after West) after a vast painting,

Cat. 64. *St. Paul Shaking the Viper from his Hand After the Shipwreck.* 1791
Engraving by Francesco Bartolozzi
Sheet: 29⅛ x 17¹⁵⁄₁₆ in. (740 x 456 mm.)
The Baltimore Museum of Art: Garrett Collection
(BMA 1946.112.14663)

twenty-five feet in height, installed behind the altar in the chapel of the Royal Naval Hospital at Greenwich in 1789— but the project for the royal chapel was on an altogether different scale, encompassing as many as thirty-six planned paintings, all of them large. It was George III's greatest

Cat. 31. *Isaiah's Lips Anointed with Fire.* (ca. 1784)
Oil on canvas. 150 x 61 in. (381.1 x 155 cm.)
Bob Jones University, Greenville, South Carolina

venture as a patron, intended to fulfill his hopes for a British school by enabling West to work on the scale of a Raphael or Michelangelo, and it was—or should have been—the central and crowning undertaking of West's career. He worked on it from 1779 to 1801 and completed eighteen paintings, but the entire scheme was never realized, and the paintings, never installed at Windsor, were returned to West's sons by George IV and dispersed by them in 1829. Cat. 31 is one of seven pictures for the chapel that have been reunited in the War Memorial Chapel of Bob Jones University in Greenville, South Carolina. Cat. 47 was left unfinished when West stopped work on the project in 1801. Cat. 38 is an oil sketch for a picture intended but never carried out for the chapel, which West did later paint as an independent work at the end of his life.

West described the series as "the progress of Revealed Religion from its commencement to its completion." The common denominator among the subjects, beyond all being biblical, is that they show moments when God's authority and will are revealed to mankind. *Noah Sacrificing* (cat. 47) is based on Genesis 8:20 through 9:17, the description of Noah's sacrificial offering after the deluge, which is terminated by the appearance of a rainbow, God's covenant with all living creatures to send no more universal floods. Cat. 31 shows an angel descending to purge the prophet Isaiah of his sins by touching a burning coal to his lips; the text is Isaiah 6:1–9. West exhibited it at the Royal Academy in 1784 as *The Call of the Prophet Isaiah* together with a *Call of the Prophet Jeremiah* of corresponding size and a larger *Moses Receiving the Laws*.[11] The three were planned as a triptych for the altar wall of the chapel, and the tall, narrow compositions used for Isaiah and Jeremiah were determined by their positions on either side. If West had carried the cycle to completion, it would have concluded with a group of pictures of the ultimate visionary revelations vouchsafed in the last book of the New Testament, The Revelation of St. John the Divine. For the chapel proper none of them went past sketches such as cat. 38 of *Death on the Pale Horse*, probably because of George III's disapproval of their content, which is discussed in the following chapter. The rest of the program had a more conservative underlying message of implicit affirmation of orthodox Anglican theology in the face of challenges from eighteenth-century Deists, who believed in God on rational grounds, but rejected testimony of divinely revealed religion.

Visions were the staple subject of Counter-Reformation baroque art, and West's use of melodramatic facial expressions, heads thrown back, and arms outflung, to express the terror, amazement, and veneration of mortals confronted by the divine, comes straight out of the baroque repertory, in one more example of his making form follow function. The visionary excitement that such images should convey is best seen in the relatively free handling of the preparatory sketches and the unfinished *Noah Sacrificing*. West had difficulties with the large scale of the finished pictures, in

Cat. 47. *Noah Sacrificing.* (ca. 1801)
Oil on canvas. 72 x 138 in. (183 x 350.7 cm.)
Collection San Antonio Museum Association,
San Antonio, Texas

Cat. 34. *Agriculture (Husbandry Aided by Arts
and Commerce).* 1789
Oil on paper mounted on panel. 20 x 24 in. (50.8 x 61 cm.), oval
Mint Museum, Charlotte, North Carolina:
Gift of the Woman's Auxiliary

Cat. 35. *Genius Calling Forth the Fine Arts to Adorn
Manufactures and Commerce*. 1789
Oil on paper. 19½ x 24¾ in. (49.5 x 62.9 cm.)
The Fine Arts Museums of San Francisco,
Gift of Mr. and Mrs. John D. Rockefeller 3rd

which problems stemming from his inadequate training became magnified, and in which, as well, he increasingly relied on studio assistants to help him cover so many square feet of canvas. He sent all the completed pictures to the Royal Academy, where they dominated the exhibitions by dint of sheer size but were universally unloved and contrasted unfavorably to the sketches.

The royal chapel, which no longer exists, was in the state apartments in the upper ward of Windsor Castle. In 1782 or 1783 West also began to design stained-glass windows of New Testament subjects for St. George's Chapel in the castle's lower ward.[12] This was work on an even larger scale, determined by the Gothic architecture of the chapel. The cartoon of the Crucifixion intended for the west window measured thirty-six by twenty-eight feet and was described in 1807 as the largest picture in the world. That window was never completed, owing to the death of the glassmaker after ten years' work on it. Four others were completed and installed, only to be destroyed in a mid-nineteenth-century restoration of the chapel. All but one of the full-sized cartoons have also disappeared or been destroyed.

Other no-longer extant works executed in another medium after West's designs were the ceiling decorations of the drawing room in the Queen's Lodge at Windsor. This was a separate structure built as a residence for the royal family by Sir William Chambers between 1778 and 1782 on the south terrace of the castle. West made oil sketches for five main oval compositions, plus numerous drawings for lesser details. The ceiling was carried out in the novel medium of colored marble dust, called *marmortinto*, in 1788 by a German confectioner named Haas, who specialized otherwise in arranging table decorations. Cats. 34 and 35, both signed and dated 1789 and exhibited in 1790 are two of the sketches, which West continued to work on after the ceiling was installed. The overall subject was an allegorical representation of British prosperity under George III. Cat. 35, exhibited with the explanatory title *Genius Calling Forth Arts and Sciences; part of a design in the Queen's Lodge, Windsor, intended to show the utility they are to this, as a commercial nation*, was the model for the central panel. Cat. 34, for one of the four corner ovals, shows *Agriculture*.

The actual panels on the ceiling may have been somewhat larger than the sketches (one source gives the dimension of three by four feet for *Genius Calling Forth Arts and Sciences*); nonetheless, they were miniscule when compared to the decorations of the Audience Chamber and the two chapels at Windsor. The playful and decorative intent, which is implied by the unusual final medium, is reflected in the colors of *Genius Calling Forth Arts and Sciences*, which have the spun-sugar lightness of icing on a cake, in contrast to the sonorous tonalities of West's contemporary historical and biblical paintings. Genius descending with the torch of enlightenment is not unrelated to the angel descending with a glowing coal to touch Isaiah in cat. 31, but he belongs to a different, carefree world. Whereas West eschewed allegory in works of greater pretension, here it is the appropriate language for a scheme in which individual pictures are subordinated to the decorative whole.

In *Genius Calling Forth Arts and Sciences* the personifications of painting, sculpture (leaning on a relief of George III), and architecture in the lower right—the arts nurtured by the Royal Academy of Arts—have pride of place. Music is in the middle distance, under Genius's left arm, and the scientific pursuits of navigation, geography, and astronomy are relegated to the sides. A telescope on the right is aimed at an *H* with a disk attached to it in the sky in the upper left: the symbol of the planet Uranus discovered in 1781 by Sir William Herschel, whose astronomical observations were generously and enthusiastically supported by George III. As a beneficiary of royal largesse, Herschel, another exact contemporary of the king, was West's scientific opposite number.

Agriculture is primarily a harvest scene and was probably partly inspired by George Stubbs's *Haymakers* and *Reapers* exhibited in 1786 (both Tate Gallery). A drawing for West's composition is dated 1787. Like Stubbs's pictures, *Agriculture* shows workers, including women, actually working, rather than in a state of pastoral ease like the rococo peasants of Boucher or Gainsborough. Also echoing Stubbs is the erect central female figure, around whom the composition revolves. Yet, unlike Stubbs's workers, West's do not wear contemporary clothes, and the painting is not a picture of a single activity or season. Ploughing, planting, and a shepherd and his flocks are visible on the left, and behind the main harvesters of grain an older man picks grapes. Next to him appears to be a pastoral poet, while a bare-bottomed child in the foreground suggests the theme of the ages of man, whose progression from infancy to ripe old age parallels that of the crops. The chief message is about fertility and abundance, traditional allegorical stuff, but included not simply because of tradition. George III was a dedicated farmer, who could stroll from his rural home in the Queen's Lodge through his own flourishing farms at Windsor, where he followed the most up-to-date practices in breeding and cultivation. Increase of agricultural productivity by scientific husbandry and efficient land use was a major public achievement during his reign. An alternative title for *Agriculture* in a list drawn up by the artist was *Husbandry Aided by Arts and Commerce*. On that list its companions, in addition to *Genius Calling Forth Arts and Sciences*, were *Manufactory Giving Support to Industry*, *The Four Quarters of the Globe Bringing Treasure to Britannia*, and *Marine and Inland Navigation Enriching Britannia*.[13] Although conceived as parts of a seemingly frivolous decorative program, such allegories, painted in the midst of the Industrial Revolution, address matters that most modern historians would consider infinitely more important than the doings of kings and princes in the more ambitious

Cat. 23. *Six Children of George III.* 1776
Oil on canvas. 66¼ x 71 in. (168.3 x 180.4 cm.)
Her Majesty Queen Elizabeth II
Copyright reserved to Her Majesty Queen Elizabeth II

Cat. 62. *George, Prince of Wales, with Prince Frederick.* 1779
Mezzotint by Valentine Green
Sheet: 25⁹⁄₁₆ x 17⁵⁄₁₆ in. (650 x 440 mm.)
The Baltimore Museum of Art: Garrett Collection
(BMA 1946.112.10498)

historical subjects West was painting at the same time.

West's role as royal portraitist from 1776 to 1783 started, conveniently, when he was receiving no royal commands for historical pictures. In the preceding decade the portrait painter most favored by the royal family had been Johann Zoffany, the German-born specialist in small-scale conversation pieces, but he left England from 1772 to 1779, forcing George III to find someone else to record his growing family. In 1772 and following years West painted a few conversation pieces, such as that of his own family (cat. 17), demonstrating his capability of filling Zoffany's place, and that is what he did until replaced in turn by Gainsborough, who started to paint royal portraits in 1781.

Six Children of George III (cat. 23) shows the six youngest members of the family as of 1776, when it was painted. The youngest, Princess Mary, was born on April 25, 1776, and a preparatory drawing for the picture, evidently made

earlier, shows only five children. On a larger scale than the usual conversation piece, it is an informal group portrait, which carries on the careful description of clothes, toys, flowers, and pets of Zoffany. West also painted a double portrait in the same year of the children's older sister Charlotte, Princess Royal, with their mother the queen, and, in 1777 and 1778, a pair of full-length double portraits of their four older brothers.[14] Cat. 62 is a mezzotint by Valentine Green (who did many prints after West; cats. 57 and 58 are also by him) after the portrait of the two oldest boys: George, Prince of Wales, at the age of seventeen, and Frederick, sixteen, the future Duke of York, Bishop of Osnabruck, and commander-in-chief of the British Army, destined to be immortalized in nursery rhyme as "the grand old Duke of York." Their great inherited positions demanded a dignity not imposed upon their happy-go-lucky siblings, and the portrait conforms to established conventions of the formal royal portrait. The Prince of Wales wears the collar of the Order of the Garter over ermine robes of state; Frederick wears the collar and robes of the Garter and, for good measure, the collar of the Order of the Bath as well. On a table to the left are a plumed hat of the Order of the Garter and the older prince's crown.

Cat. 28 is the first of two portraits of the queen painted in 1779 and 1782, the second being a remarkable mirror reversal of the first, repeating all but incidental details. In the foreground the crown and ermine robes are signs of position, but the background is more personal. In the distance is a view of the Queen's Lodge, her new country home, with the larger mass of Windsor Castle looming over it, and in the intervening space are the royal children, thirteen in the picture of 1779, fourteen in 1782, following the birth of Prince Alfred in 1780. Another adjustment between the two versions, presumably also dictated by the passage of time, is a change of royal pets at the queen's feet, the spaniel lying on the floor in the earlier picture being replaced by an apparently younger dog with different markings, who sits rather than lies. Continuity—or a demonstration of the artist's lack of imagination—is provided by Prince Augustus, who reclines on the ground before his brothers and sisters, with a dog before him, in a position similar to his position in cat. 23 of 1776, in which he throws a ball to another, smaller dog.

Sadly, the two youngest children in the portrait of 1782, Alfred and Octavius, born in 1779, died within nine months of one another, in August 1782 and May 1783 respectively. The death of the latter deeply affected the king, whose lament, "there will be no Heaven for me, if Octavius is not there," seems to have prompted two literal gestures of reassurance from West. He included a portrait of Octavius among the seraphim and cherubim of the heavenly host in his stained-glass window of the *Resurrection* in St. George's Chapel. And his last commissioned royal portrait, *The Apotheosis of Prince Alfred and Prince Octavius*, painted in 1783, shows the prince on a cloud above his terrestrial

Cat. 28. *Queen Charlotte*. 1779
Oil on canvas. 100½ x 72 in. (255.4 x 183 cm.)
Her Majesty Queen Elizabeth II

Cat. 63. *The Apotheosis of Prince Alfred
and Prince Octavius*. 1786
Engraving by Robert Strange
Sheet: 24½ x 17¾ in. (623 x 451 mm.)
The Metropolitan Museum of Art:
Gift of Georgiana W. Sargent
in memory of John Osborne Sargent, 1924

home, the Queen's Lodge, being welcomed to heaven by the younger brother who had predeceased him. The engraving after it (cat. 63) was the only print after the work of a living artist made by the eminent engraver and former Jacobite Robert Strange, who presented the plate and a large number of impressions to the bereaved king and queen and received a knighthood in return. The portrait is allegorical but the image of two children lovingly tended by an angel is Christian, rather than classical as in *Mr. and Mrs. Custance* (cat. 26) of five years before, reflecting West's turn away from classical subjects in the 1780's. The painting appeared in the same Royal Academy exhibition of 1784 as West's picture of Isaiah and an angel (cat. 31).

Further tragedy struck the royal family in 1788 when George III was laid low by his first attack of apparent insanity (now generally diagnosed as a congenital disease named porphyria), from which he recovered the following spring. *His Majesty George III Resuming Power in 1789* (cat.

36) shows him walking allegorically away from the doctors who had nursed him back to health, to reclaim the crown and throne from the prime minister, the younger William Pitt, and other leaders of the government, who had guarded them during his incapacity. The column behind the doctors has the word *SCIENCE* inscribed on the abacus and carries a shield recording the date, March 10, 1789, when the king resumed his official duties by opening parliament. The two columns on the left, inscribed *HONOR* and *VIRTUE*, bear shields recording votes in the Houses of Lords and Commons supporting the king in a dispute over a proposed regency. Queen Charlotte stands behind her husband, and behind her is Windsor Castle, to which the king returned on March 14 amidst great rejoicing. In the sky, a faintly discernible eye of providence sends down rays of light upon the king.

Unlike the works previously discussed in this chapter, *George III Resuming Power* was not a royal commission. It incorporates elements of a transparency that West displayed before his house in Windsor on the night of the king's return, and West undoubtedly hoped to be asked to perpetuate his celebration of the happy event in permanent fashion. The king, on the other hand, may have been understandably unenthusiastic about owning a constant reminder of the terrifying collapse that had gone before, but, additionally, his collapse signaled the beginning of the end of West's position at court. As early as 1793 comments were heard that he did not go to Windsor as often as before.[15] In contrast to the multiplicity of his undertakings in the 1780's, West received no new royal commissions after 1789, although he did continue to design windows for St. George's Chapel and to produce paintings for the royal chapel until 1801. As George III became less and less able to make decisions, the queen, who was no friend of West, made them for him. When the ceiling decorations in the Queen's Lodge were first put up, they were immediately taken down at her instruction during the king's first illness in 1788–1789, only to be hurriedly put up again before his return to Windsor. During a later illness in 1801, the queen ordered that West cease work on the chapel pictures, and following the king's final breakdown, which necessitated establishment of a regency in 1811, his stipend from the crown came to an end. But during the 1790's West had difficulties with the king as well, and in 1794 he told Joseph Farington of his distress about the king's "having been informed of his holding democratic principles."[16] The atmosphere of reactionary panic provoked by revolutionary France—Louis XVI died on the guillotine and England and France went to war in 1793—engendered suspicions that the earlier conflict with West's revolutionary American compatriots surprisingly had not, but George III was right to question his loyalty. Although West was neither hypocritical nor opportunistic in working for the king, running through his paintings of the 1770's, 1780's, and 1790's are undercurrents of meaning that proclaim dubious reverence for the institution of monarchy.

Cat. 36. *His Majesty George III Resuming Power in 1789.*
(ca. 1789)
Oil on canvas. 20⁷⁄₁₆ x 30¼ in. (51.9 x 76.9 cm.)
Hirschl & Adler Galleries, Inc., New York

Cat. 65. *King Lear: Act III, Scene IV (King Lear in the Storm).* 1793
Engraving by William Sharp
Sheet: 21¹⁄₁₆ x 27⁹⁄₁₆ in. (535 x 700 mm.)
The Baltimore Museum of Art: Garrett Collection
(BMA 1946.112.8036)

In May 1789, while West was probably working on *George III Resuming Power*, the Boydell Shakespeare Gallery opened. This was an ambitious venture by the print seller John Boydell, whose profits from prints such as that of *The Death of General Wolfe* (cat. 61) paid for it, to support the English school by commissioning and exhibiting pictures illustrating the most admired of English authors, and then publishing engravings after them. Cat. 65 is the engraving after West's *King Lear in the Storm* (Museum of Fine Arts, Boston), the first of two subjects he painted for the gallery. While the large painting was on view in Boydell's exhibition, in what seems like an astonishingly insensitive act, West also sent an oil sketch of the composition to the Royal Academy.[17] Although the subject must have been chosen and the composition designed well before the onset of the king's attacks of delirium in October 1788, and although the treatment is not unsympathetic toward Lear, it nonetheless depicts a mad king. And since it was not painted for George III, its histrionic frenzy perhaps embodies West's deeply-felt attitude more truly than the measured stride of his recently deranged monarch's return to duty in the respectful and pompous commemoration intended for official consumption. Similar obliquely subversive allusions pervade his pictures of biblical subjects.

Cat. 38. *Death on the Pale Horse.* 1796
Oil on canvas. 23½ x 50½ in. (59.7 x 128.3 cm.)
The Detroit Institute of Arts:
Founders Society Purchase,
Robert H. Tannahill Foundation Fund

6. Revelation and Revolution

Saul and the Witch of Endor of 1777 (cat. 25) derives from the twenty-eighth chapter of the first book of Samuel. Saul has gone to a witch to try to learn the outcome of a forthcoming battle with the Philistines. Upon her evocation of the spirit of Saul's deceased predecessor, "Saul perceived that it was Samuel, and stooped with his face to the ground, and bowed himself." The subject of the painting is the response to the ghostly apparition of Saul and his two frightened companions, who flee through the door behind him. As such, it is a textbook example of the sublime, a concept given currency in late eighteenth-century England by Edmund Burke's *Philosophical Enquiry into the Origins of Our Ideas of the Sublime and the Beautiful* published in 1757. This enquiry defined sublimity as the opposite of beauty, but bearing an equal aesthetic power, which stems from our psychological responses to what we perceive as threatening. In the 1770's and 1780's a generation of artists, among them John Hamilton Mortimer, Joseph Wright of Derby, Henry Fuseli, and West, devoted themselves to images of violent struggles, terrifying apparitions, and the like, putting into practice Burke's ideas, which by 1775, according to a recent scholar, "were as generally familiar as Freud's are today."[1] They were all more or less inspired by seventeenth-century paintings of such subjects by Salvator Rosa, and West's *Saul and the Witch of Endor* is an updated version of Salvator's *Saul and the Witch of Endor* in the Louvre, as are treatments of the subject by Mortimer, Fuseli, and William Blake. Since the theory of sublimity was about responses, many pictures of sublime subjects show not only something to terrify us, but include within the picture awe-stricken observers such as Saul and his companions, whose reactions we can observe.

This new content in West's art of the 1770's was not dictated by his choosing to paint an Old Testament subject. *Jacob Blessing the Sons of Joseph* of circa 1766 (cat. 8), which is also from the Old Testament, shows a gentle domestic narrative with none of the frightening dimensions of *Saul*

and the Witch of Endor. On the other hand, the Bible does present countless supernatural apparitions, several of which West subsequently was to paint as components of "the progress of Revealed Religion" for the royal chapel at Windsor. As evidenced by Isaiah in cat. 31 and Noah in cat. 47, the series' human participants are treated to a cornucopia of sublime manifestations of the Divine Will, encouraging the suspicion that in 1779 currently popular notions inspired by Burke were as important as theology in prompting West to conceive his great undertaking devoted to biblical revelation.

From Saul to Noah, the protagonists of West's later biblical pictures are very different from his earlier Agrippina and Regulus. They are not actors, but witnesses of things more important than themselves. They are neither philosophical nor heroic and seem to have no choices other than awe, obedience, and shame. Instead of being examples of virtuous behavior, they are, by and large, sinners, whose humiliation and punishment provide our instruction. The intellectual context is less the spirit of tolerant and rational enquiry of the eighteenth-century enlightenment than the hell-fire fundamentalism of the religious revivals of the nineteenth century or of earlier Puritanism. Apart from the pharaoh in two chapel pictures, the sinners are not regal in the pictures West painted for George III, but in other pictures he painted not only Saul before Samuel, but also David chastised by Nathan, and Belshazzar harangued by Daniel in works exhibited in 1775 and 1776.[2] West did not invent the subjects, but, since these works were not commissioned (one he sold in 1779, and two were in his studio sale in 1829), he chose them. All three show bad kings listening to prophets pointing out their sins, not the most politic subjects for the king's Historical Painter to paint in his free time.

What Saul also hears from Samuel is that he will lose his kingdom in the next day's battle. That happens, and Saul, his three sons, and all his men are killed. In 1777 George III was waging war with his American colonies, and on

Cat. 25. *Saul and the Witch of Endor.* 1777
Oil on canvas. 20½ x 27 in. (52.1 x 68.6 cm.)
Wadsworth Atheneum, Hartford:
Bequest of Mrs. Clara Hinton Gould

October 17, his army suffered a humiliating defeat at Saratoga, in what was instantly and widely recognized as the turning point of the war. We do not know if West painted the picture after news of the defeat reached London, when he could hardly have failed to recognize the parallel. If painted before, the picture had its own prophetic dimension, one that might seem coincidental, but for true believers prophecies fulfilled are not coincidences. West did not just happen to paint Belshazzar in 1776 and Saul in 1777. The outbreak of war on his native soil had to affect him, and his inevitable conflict of loyalties was reflected in his art, albeit in ways he may not have always acknowledged to himself. He did not exhibit *Saul and the Witch of Endor*, possibly out of fear that it would be perceived as disloyal, but it was engraved after the close of the American war by William Sharp, a radical republican, who was arrested in 1794 for his beliefs. Sharp also engraved West's *King Lear in the Storm* (cat. 65).

In 1777 West painted a large altarpiece of *St. Michael* for Trinity College in Cambridge. Cat. 22, signed and dated 1776, is the preparatory oil sketch. The subject comes from Revelation 20:1–3, which describes an angel coming down from heaven with a great chain and casting Satan into the bottomless pit. There is no remarkable originality in the subject; James Barry had previously designed a *St. Michael* for the aborted project for St. Paul's and further back lay famous St. Michaels by Raphael and Guido Reni. Nevertheless, West's paintings of an armed angel in hostile conflict with a monstrous demon were painted at a time when armed hostilities were underway in America. The master of Trinity College, who commissioned the altarpiece, Dr. John Hinchliffe, was also Bishop of Peterborough, which entitled him to a seat in the House of Lords. There he had taken an outspoken stand in 1775 in favor of coercion against the American colonies. Since this image of biblical coercion was made for him, he presumably dictated its subject, which appears to make West's radiant St. Michael stand for England, and his Satan the seditious American colonies. That alignment of the forces of good and evil is the diametrical opposite of the one implicit in *Saul and the Witch of Endor*, but St. Michael and Satan may not have meant the same things to the artist as they did to Dr. Hinchliffe. In 1775 West wrote to Charles Willson Peale:

> The present commotions between this country and its colonies is a subject I could dwell long on, but prudence and the times will not permit my saying any thing on that head—as what I might say would have but little weight in the scale of opinions. If it would, I should stand forth and speak it boldly, though it were at the risk of my all. . . . Measures taken here relative to America show but little knowledge of that country . . .and should measures with you be as wrongly advised as with us, both countries are for some time undone.[3]

He continued to be verbally circumspect, but his sympathies certainly veered toward the American side as hopes of reconciliation evaporated.

Everything in West's background, as well as his position at court, should have made him a loyalist. His old patron and friend, Chief Justice Allen of Pennsylvania, fled America and the Revolution in 1776; his fellow-student from Provost Smith's circle, Jacob Duché, came in 1777; John Singleton Copley in 1774. Yet West never aligned himself with them. While Dr. Hinchliffe may have been anti-American, other important patrons at the same time such as Dr. Thomas Wilson, the rector of St. Stephen Walbrook in London, for whom West painted a larger altarpiece in 1776,[4] were equally fervent advocates of the revolutionary cause. And, counterbalancing the loyalist exiles, West's friends also included Englishmen such as the Reverend Samuel Preston of Chevening in Kent, who bequeathed his books to the Library Company of Philadelphia (with which his only known connection was West) after writing to its directors in 1783 congratulating them on the exploits of their fellow citizens.[5] West's own pride in those exploits was manifested in his plan of 1783 to paint the great events of the revolutionary war.[6]

The Trinity College altarpiece, based on Revelation, was followed in 1779 by sketches of five subjects from Revelation included in a preliminary drawing for the royal chapel at Windsor. In 1783 West made a large drawing that he exhibited in 1784 under the title *The Triumph of Death, from the Revelations*.[7] He painted an oil sketch of the same composition in 1796, which he exhibited as *The opening of the four seals* (cat. 38), identifying it, like the earlier drawing, as for the Windsor chapel. At the end of his life he returned to the composition once again to paint a huge picture now in the Pennsylvania Academy of the Fine Arts, which he called *Death on the Pale Horse*,[8] the title by which all three versions are now generally known. A still more familiar title for what is shown, but which West did not use, is "The Four Horsemen of the Apocalypse." The opening of the four seals referred to in 1796 occurs in the sixth chapter. As each seal is opened, a horseman on a different colored horse appears to spread pestilence, famine, and destruction. The fourth horse is pale, "and his name that sat on him was Death, and Hell followed with him. And power was given unto them over the fourth part of the earth, to kill with sword, and with hunger, and with death, and with beasts of the earth."

Cat. 38 shows the first three horsemen on the right; Death on his pale horse in the center followed by a train of demons in the sky; and his victims, dying from the sword, plague, starvation, and vicious animals, below him and to the left. The best-known earlier depiction of the subject is Dürer's wood engraving of *The Four Horsemen of the Apocalypse* of circa 1496, which West evidently knew, but did not imitate. Closer at hand, John Hamilton Mortimer exhibited a drawing of the fourth horseman in 1775. However, the strongest

visual affinities of West's *Death on the Pale Horse* are not with depictions of the same or related subjects, but with the hunting scenes of Rubens. The pale horse and his rider are descendants of a horse and rider in Rubens's *Wolf and Fox Hunt* (The Metropolitan Museum of Art, New York), and the turbulent intertwining of man and beast and lurid colors bring to a Rubensian baroque crescendo West's abandonment of the sober clarity of his neoclassical works of a quarter of a century before. The eruption of irrational, visionary violence equally denies and assaults the philosophic ideals enshrined in those works.

This version of *Death on the Pale Horse* was seen at the Royal Academy in 1796 by William Beckford, the immensely wealthy and self-indulgent heir to a Jamaican sugar fortune, who was in the process of building the most extravagant single monument of the Gothic Revival, Fonthill Abbey in Wiltshire. Beckford soon began to pay West a second annual stipend equal to the king's, for which he was to receive paintings and designs for stained glass for a Revelation Chamber to contain his tomb. *St. Michael and the Dragon* (cat. 45) appeared at the Royal Academy in 1797, where it was identified as for a window at Fonthill. *The Beast Riseth Out of the Sea* (cat. 42) is one of four related sketches, which were exhibited the following year with Fonthill again cited in the catalogue, but without indication if they were for paintings or glass. After this burst of activity, no window was produced after the *St. Michael*, although one was after a companion *St. Thomas à Becket*,[9] and the Revelation Chamber never came into being. Rather than surrounding his tomb with stained glass or apocalyptic paintings, Beckford kept the sketches, possibly because he realized that they were masterpieces, which would only be diluted by further work. As early as November 1797, James Wyatt, the architect of Fonthill, told Joseph Farington that Beckford liked West's sketches, "but not his pictures, and wished him to make them like his sketches as he can."[10] Much later, in 1838, Beckford discussed with a friend the sketch of *Death on the Pale Horse*, which he had seen in 1796 but never owned, as "one of the finest things in existence," and they lamented the pains West took in finishing his large pictures: "The consequence was that the original spirit evaporated long before the completion of the great tame painting."[11]

Beckford's *St. Michael and the Dragon* is not based on the same passage from Revelation as the earlier depiction of Michael for Trinity College (cat. 22), but based on chapter twelve, in which St. Michael casts out the great red dragon and his angels, but the subjects are similar enough to demonstrate the later work's more complex, agitated, highly-colored, and melodramatic imagery. The earlier Michael

remains coolly detached, his superiority proclaimed by his classically Raphaelesque perfection, whereas his successor is more engaged in the struggle. Nevertheless, both are victors in clear-cut triumphs of good over evil, heaven over hell.

The Beast Riseth Out of the Sea illustrates a more opaque vision from the thirteenth chapter. On the left is the beast from the sea; as described in the chapter's opening verses, he has seven heads, ten horns, ten crowns upon his horns, likeness to a leopard, the feet of a bear, and mouth of a lion. He speaks blasphemies and is given power over all kindreds, tongues, and nations. In the lower right is a second beast, introduced in verse eleven, who comes out of the earth, has two horns like a lamb, speaks like a dragon, makes fire come down from heaven, and causes dwellers on the earth, led by a groveling king in the lower left, to worship the first beast. In the upper left, a third monster with a scaly red body and a long red tail is the great red dragon from chapter twelve, who is described there as possessing seven heads, ten horns, and seven crowns. Revelation 13:2 states that the dragon gave "his power, and his seat, and great authority" to the beast from the sea; those gifts are represented by the scepter which he passes to the beast, and the crown which he holds aloft. Whatever theological interpretations can be extracted from the biblical text, West's painting takes the form of yet another comment on monarchy. The crowns owe their presence to the seventeen described in Revelation, but no scepter is mentioned there, nor kings among the dwellers on earth. According to some Protestant interpretations, the beasts represent the alliance of the Church of Rome with secular power, but in 1794 the self-proclaimed prophet Richard Brothers declared that the beast rising from the sea stood for the British monarchy.[12] In West's picture, the crowned lion's head, looking for all the world like the crowned lion on the English royal crest, makes such an association seem the more likely.

Brothers also claimed that chapter six of Revelation, the source of *Death on the Pale Horse*, "relates to the present war—its progress—and consequences." That war with France, which commenced in 1793, was caricatured as an apocalyptic vision by James Gillray in a print inspired by Brothers entitled *Presages of the Millenium*, in which the pale horse ridden by the prime minister, Pitt, is the white horse of Hanover, identifiable by a royal crown on his saddle blanket.[13] This print was not based on West, as other prints by Gillray were, but its publication in 1795, with the appropriate lines from Revelation printed in its caption, seems of more than coincidental relevance to West's return to the subject, which he had previously drawn in 1783. The four horsemen of the apocalypse have been symbols of war for centuries, and the entire book of Revelation, pervaded by visions of violent conflict, has been explained as alluding to persecution and war at the time it was written. Although apocalyptic subjects foretelling the end of the world were common in

Cat. 45. *St. Michael and the Dragon*. (ca. 1797)
Oil on canvas. 50½ x 23⅜ in. (128.3 x 59.9 cm.)
The Toledo Museum of Art: Museum Purchase Fund

Cat. 42. *The Beast Riseth Out of the Sea.* 1797
Oil on panel. 31½ x 21½ in. (80 x 54.6 cm.)
Collection Thomas and Margaret McCormick,
Norton, Massachusetts

medieval art—in Romanesque sculpture and the Beatus manuscripts of tenth- and eleventh-century Spain—they gradually disappeared in the increasingly rational and secular ambience of post-Renaissance western Europe, only to resurface dramatically in the wake of the French Revolution, which was immediately interpreted as fulfilling the prophecies of Revelation. West's first apocalyptic works dating from 1776 (cat. 22) and 1779 (the first sketches for the royal chapel), done by an expatriated American during the American revolutionary war, were undertaken in an earlier but analogous historical context. He included a tiny *Death on the Pale Horse* in the sketches of 1779 and produced his first large drawing of the subject in 1783, the year that the revolutionary war came to a formal end. He then put the subject aside to take it up again in 1796 in a time of war, and he commenced his last large version in 1815, the year of the Battle of Waterloo. In that version he added a detail not in the earlier treatments, of a British victory under Richard Coeur-de-Lion over the Saracens, which a contemporary described as a "just compliment to British valour." Whether British valor was uppermost in his mind in 1796 when he painted the present *Death on the Pale Horse*, or in 1797 when he painted the second *St. Michael and the Dragon* (cat. 45), is open to question. The former is certainly more about suffering than valor. The latter could stand for Britain triumphing over the horrors unleashed by the French Revolution, but in light of the rumors in circulation in 1794 about West's "democratic principles" and in light of what *The Beast Riseth Out of the Sea* seems to show, Michael may more likely represent the new order vanquishing the infamies of the ancien régime.

The equation of contemporary revolution and Revelation is emphatically drawn in the prophetic books of William Blake, among them *America, a Prophecy* of 1793, of which he is said to have presented a copy to West. Blake and West as artists seem worlds apart, but in 1798 a close friend of Blake's, the miniature painter Ozias Humphrey, told Joseph Farington that *The Beast Riseth Out of the Sea* was the "finest conception ever come from the mind of man." West is recorded as having praised Blake's designs as "works of extraordinary genius and imagination" in February 1796, at a time when he may have been working on the sketch of *Death on the Pale Horse* (cat. 38), which he exhibited two months later. After 1800 Blake painted some of his greatest watercolors showing identical subjects from Revelation as West's paintings of the 1790's, which, at the least, provided him significant iconographical guideposts. Stylistically, the Rubensian *Death on the Pale Horse* of 1796 also provides a foretaste of the neobaroque style of the French Romantic artist Eugène Delacroix, who was to see and admire West's paintings on a visit to London in 1825; a note on one of his studies for *The Death of Sardanapalus* of 1827 (Louvre) says "étudier les croquis de West."[14] But cross-channel contact was also made earlier, when West visited Paris during the Peace of Amiens of 1802, the one brief respite in the constant state of war from 1793 to 1814 between England and France. The president of the Royal Academy went as an honored guest, and he took with him the sketch of *Death on the Pale Horse*, which was hung in the Salon of 1802. There Napoleon Bonaparte himself tried to buy it, and it received considerable attention otherwise, including both criticism as a "caricature of Rubens" and praise for the execution from David. Whether its public exhibition in Paris could have significantly affected the course of French art, as has been claimed, seems unlikely. Contemporary pictures by David's former students Girodet and Gros departed equally dramatically from the neoclassicism of their master, and, at most, sight of West's picture confirmed the validity of what they were already doing, rather than pointing them in new directions.[15] In Paris, West and William Sharp, the radical engraver, annoyed their fellow English visitor Farington by comparing the improved lot of the French since the Revolution to the condition of the London poor.[16] After returning to London, West's undisguised admiration for Napoleon became one more source of irritation for George III.[17]

7. Into the Nineteenth Century

West's election in 1792 as president of the Royal Academy, making him titular head of the British school in succession to Sir Joshua Reynolds, ironically came at a time when his position at court was beginning to slip and when his critical reputation was about to start into a long decline. The fall from critical favor of someone who had been a visible and powerful presence as long as West was perhaps inevitable. An artist who came to maturity in the third quarter of the eighteenth century had to address different concerns and speak a different language than Turner, Constable, Haydon, or Wilkie, artists of the nineteenth century born after *The Departure of Regulus from Rome* and *The Death of General Wolfe* were part of history. To many critics from their generation such as William Hazlitt, born in 1778, who in 1814 dismissed West with the comment, "He is only great by the acre,"[1] monumental public art in the tradition of Raphael no longer was the ultimate goal to which the national school should aspire as it had been in 1768 for the founders of the Royal Academy.

West, on the other hand, remained committed to such works, and the main achievements of the final, nineteenth-century phase of his career were three huge religious paintings. The second, *Christ Rejected*[2]—measuring 200 by 260 inches, or almost twenty-one feet across—was completed and exhibited in 1814, the year of Hazlitt's "great by the acre." The third, a monumental treatment—twenty-five feet in width—of *Death on the Pale Horse*[3] based on the oil sketch of 1796 (cat. 38) appeared in 1817 as the old artist's last significant undertaking. Without the royal patronage that had sustained him from 1768 to 1810, West painted these two vast works on his own initiative and did not sell them. Instead, he exhibited them in a specially rented gallery in Pall Mall and charged admission at the door. Almost a quarter of a million viewers were reported to have paid a shilling apiece to see *Christ Rejected*. Thus at the end of his

life, West achieved a truly public art, paid for by the public itself rather than by a public-spirited royal patron.

The first of the trio of late paintings, *Christ Healing the Sick in the Temple* (see cat. 69), whose success inspired the other two, was undertaken under other circumstances, but equally independent of the royal and aristocratic patronage that had provided most of West's income since his arrival in England. In 1800 the Pennsylvania Hospital in Philadelphia wrote to West asking for the gift of a painting. Although it took him over a decade, he painted *Christ Healing the Sick* in response. It was thus conceived as a charitable contribution destined for America, his first work, except for portraits, painted after half a century in England for his native land. But it never got to Philadelphia. Upon its completion in March 1811, the British Institution, a body formed in 1805 by wealthy collectors primarily to organize exhibitions, purchased it to be the first work in a proposed national gallery. West then painted a slightly larger repetition of the composition for the Pennsylvania Hospital, where it finally arrived in 1817 and where it remains.[4] When the English National Gallery came into being in the 1820's, the first *Christ Healing the Sick* did go there. It was subsequently transferred to the Tate Gallery and damaged beyond repair by a flood in 1928, but its appearance is known from the engraving by Charles Heath (cat. 69).

What induced West to sell the painting was an offer of 3,000 guineas, which was far higher than anything he had previously received, and was widely reported as the most money ever paid to any artist for a single work of art. Not only did it constitute tangible recognition of West's stature, but news of it guaranteed large public attendance when the painting went on view at the British Institution, which had so many paid admissions that it made a tidy profit from its purchase. For West, at precisely the moment when his £1,000 a year from the crown came to an end, such monetary

Cat. 48. *Robert Fulton*. 1806
Oil on canvas. 35½ x 27½ in. (90.2 x 69.9 cm.)
New York State Historical Association, Cooperstown
©New York State Historical Association, Cooperstown, N.Y.

success prompted ideas about the sequels which would occupy him for the rest of his working life. By July 1811 he had prepared an oil sketch (cat. 52) for the even larger *Christ Rejected*, which he then spent the next three years painting.

Christ Healing the Sick illustrates lines from Matthew:

> And the blind and the lame came to him in the Temple, and he healed them
> And when the Chief Priests and Scribes saw the wonderful things that he did, and the children crying in the Temple, and saying, Hosanna to the son of David; they were sore displeased (21:14–15).

Christ Rejected shows an incident recorded in all four Gospels. A catalogue published by West in 1814 described the subject as "Christ rejected by the Jewish High Priest, the Elders, and the People when brought to them by Pilate from the Judgment Hall." West developed the composition of *Christ Healing the Sick* from sketches originally made for the royal chapel at Windsor, a procedure he would follow again for his final *Death on the Pale Horse*. *Christ Rejected*, on the contrary, shows a subject he had not previously treated. Commenced when he was seventy-three years old, it was his last work to be begun and carried through on a monumental scale. To the already elaborate composition worked out in the oil sketch, he added more figures and details to the large painting to its detriment. While it was still on view in its own exhibition, West sent the sketch to the Royal Academy in 1815, where one critic proclaimed it "decidedly superior to the picture itself," and the connoisseur, collector, and future benefactor of the National Gallery, Sir George Beaumont, declared it the one work there to show "the true quality of art, . . . the comprehensiveness and completeness which is found in the work of the great masters." The catalogue accompanying the large picture claimed, "to excite feelings in the spectator similar to those produced by perusal of the Sacred texts. . . . The delineation of nearly the whole scale of human passions, from the basest to those which partake most of the divine nature, has thus been necessarily attempted." What that meant was a visual sermon declaimed in readily grasped language analogous to that of popular revivalist preachers. When Joseph Farington visited the exhibition in October 1814 he found about eighty people, who "appeared to be impressed with much awe by the subject. It was like a small congregation in a Church."[5] West's catalogue described the composition as "epic," a word he previously had used in justifying the liberties with historical fact in pictures such as *The Death of General Wolfe*. To an unsympathetic critic such as Hazlitt such claims amounted to little more than a preference for quantity over quality.

If Hazlitt was consistently severe, the cruelest of all criticism came from Lord Byron as part of a denunciation of the seventh Earl of Elgin's removal to England of most of the sculptures from the Parthenon, in which Byron saw West, who proselytized for the purchase of the sculptures for the British Museum, as an accomplice:

> Meanwhile, the flattering, feeble dotard West,
> Europe's worst dauber, and poor Britain's best,
> With palsied hand shall turn each model o'er,
> And own himself an infant of fourscore.

What prompted Byron's scurrility was the old artist's geniune excitement about the sculptures.[6] After first seeing the Elgin marbles in the winter of 1808, he told Joseph Farington that he wished he was twenty years old again, so "that he might labor to profit by them." Despite being seventy instead of twenty, he did so labor in the summer of 1808, when with Benjamin Robert Haydon, almost fifty years his junior, he was the first artist in England to make copies after the sculptures. To the parliamentary committee considering the purchase of the marbles he testified in 1816 that *Christ Healing the Sick* and *Christ Rejected* demonstrated what he had learned from them.

The *Angel of the Resurrection* (cat. 66) is a concrete example of West's receptivity to new stimuli of another sort. Made in 1801 for a demonstration publication titled *Specimens of Polyautography*, it was the first work done anywhere by an artist of stature in the new medium of lithography invented by Aloys Senefelder in 1798. The lithographic crayon allowed the print to retain some of the freshness and energy of a drawn sketch, and the youthful angel, coming for once as a bearer of good news—"He is not here: for he is risen"—seems happily appropriate to a publication announcing a newly invented medium at the beginning of a new century.

Responsiveness to new stimuli is also embodied in West's double portrait of his two sons (cat. 40) and in *Cicero Discovering the Tomb of Archimedes* (cat. 43), dated 1796 and 1797 respectively and both exhibited at the Royal Academy in 1797. In 1795 a father and daughter named Provis approached West with a formula or process that they claimed to have found in an old book from Italy.[7] The process's main components were a dark absorbent ground and a universal shadow of "Titian shade," made up of dark lake, indigo, and ivory black. The two pictures were painted as experiments using it, and both are extraordinary in effect due to what a contemporary critic described as "a dark and purpurine hue," the perhaps inevitable result of the dark ground and Titian shade. *Cicero Discovering the Tomb of Archimedes* was West's most substantial work in the process, and before the exhibition of 1797 he told Farington, "Much had been talked of the Picture, but the Artists will be astonished when they see it." They were, but not quite in the way he expected. One called the picture black, and another described it as a moonlight landscape with figures in the sun. In reply West told Farington, "it was very odd,—it looked bright at home," and added, "the process is excellent but is not yet fully understood." However, he soon decided that Provis's grounds were too cold and too

Cat. 52. *Study for Christ Rejected.* 1811
Oil on paper mounted on panel
30¼ x 42¼ in. (76.9 x 107.4 cm.)
Memorial Art Gallery of the University of Rochester:
Marion Stratton Gould Fund
©Memorial Art Gallery of the University of Rochester

He is not here : for he is risen. &c.

Cat. 66. *Angel of the Resurrection*. 1801
Lithograph by Benjamin West
12⁷⁄₁₆ x 9 in. (316 x 229 mm.)
National Gallery of Art, Washington:
Rosenwald Collection, 1947.7.135

purple, and he modified the process in his next attempt, *A Bacchante* (cat. 41), dated 1797 and exhibited in 1798. Farington reported in August 1797, "West has painted a Bacchante on a Buff-Col'd. ground, adhering *to the process* except in Flesh which in the body colour becomes a contrast which He thinks luminous—He says 'twas the way of Titian—the other *process that* of Bassan." While experimenting with the process in 1796, West managed to alienate both the Provises, who accused him of trying to cheat them, and his fellow artists, who referred to it as the Venetian Secret and suspected that he was monopolizing it for his own advantage. In January 1797 the Provises made the secret available to anyone for a fee of ten guineas. West predicted that it would form a new epoch in the art, but his difficulties in making the process work were more accurately prophetic, and it was rapidly forgotten.

The terms "Venetian Secret" and "Titian shade" are indicative not only of qualities the artists sought to achieve by using the process, but also of the historical, old-masterly nature of their ambitions. The notion of rediscovering the Venetian Secret had enhanced allure in 1796 and 1797 because, owing to the abundance of works entering England in the aftermath of the French Revolution, the collecting of old pictures acquired a frenetic energy during the decade. Although many artists resented the increased interest in earlier pictures at the expense of contemporary works, West was quoted as saying,

> that next to the merit of having painted a picture which should bring honor to the art, and become an ornament to the state wherein it was produced, was the credit of having brought from foreign countries works of the great masters. The importation of such works tends to enrich the nation which receives them, it holds out a bright example for imitation, and rouses and calls into action the native talents of those who feel the sacred flame of emulation.[8]

This attitude must have been fueled by memory of the absence of examples for imitation in colonial Pennsylvania. West was active as an expert advising on acquisitions and occasionally as a restorer, and he formed a large collection of his own. The most important group of pictures ever to come en masse to England was the collection of the Dukes of Orléans, dispersed in 1792, of which endless echoes can be found in West's later works. The pose of his *Bacchante* is adapted from a Titian of a girl holding a tray of fruit, traditionally called *Titian's Daughter*, and both *Christ Healing the Sick* and *Christ Rejected* owed debts to the largest and most celebrated of the Orléans pictures, the *Raising of Lazarus* by Sebastiano del Piombo (now in the National Gallery, London), which West praised in 1796 as the finest picture in the world, and which he retouched in 1798.[9]

He had time for such activities after 1790 and probably need for the income they produced, because of the falling off of his royal commissions. During the latter 1780's his energies were focused on his projects at Windsor and a handful of other major works, but in the 1790's his output was much more diverse. Not only did he return to types of pictures—classical subjects and portraits—that he had virtually abandoned in the preceding decade, but he also took up new ones, including informal genre scenes, which seem the antithesis of everything he hitherto stood for.

Cat. 41. *A Bacchante.* 1797
Oil on canvas. 50 x 40 in. (127.1 x 101.6 cm.)
Collection Muriel and Philip Berman,
Allentown, Pennsylvania

When *A Drayman Drinking* of 1796 (cat. 39) appeared at the Royal Academy in 1797, one critic did ask whether such works were appropriate for the president of the Royal Academy, but concluded that the artist indulged himself "in a familiar incident" as a form of relaxation. West took a more practical view. Although he could have sold *A Drayman Drinking*, he told Farington that he would not sell any of his small pictures, but intended to make a collection of them to sell together, "to make an independence for others." Unlike ambitious history paintings, genre scenes on a modest scale did have a ready market, and West must have been inspired to think in such terms by the commercial success of paintings of humble subjects by George Morland and Francis Wheatley. *A Drayman Drinking*, however, reflects the more immediate influence of a series of urban scenes of draymen and horses by the animal painter George Garrard, most of them painted for the brewer Samuel Whitbread,[10]

Cat. 39. *A Drayman Drinking.* 1796
Oil on canvas. 15½ x 21 in. (39.4 x 53.4 cm.)
Collection Dr. and Mrs. Henry C. Landon III

Cat. 46. *The Sun Setting Behind a Group of Trees on the Banks
of the Thames at Twickenham.* 1799(?)
Oil on slate. 12 x 17 in. (30.5 x 43.2 cm.)
The Charles P. Russell Collection of Deerfield Academy,
Deerfield, Massachusetts

whose product "Entire" (more commonly known as "porter") is advertised over the alehouse door in West's picture. Recruiting posters for the army and navy on the same wall reflect the state of war between England and France in 1796 and suggest a topical message implicit in the "familiar incident." The king's name on the most legibly inscribed sign and the dome of St. Paul's on the horizon emphatically establish the setting, and the activity constitutes a microcosm of peaceful, industrious, and prosperous English life. In addition to the drayman, whose face is buried in a tankard, the two other main figures are carrying and stacking bricks evidently intended for the building under the scaffolding on the left. The scene of beer drinking depends upon Hogarth's famous celebration of beer as the cornerstone of a thriving city in his engraving *Beer Street*, which had as a foil the evils shown in the companion print of *Gin Lane*. West painted no companion picture, but the historical foil to his depiction of English tranquility was the revolutionary turmoil of contemporary France. Indeed a Hogarthian and grotesquely savage picture of wine-drinking *sans-culottes*, *Plundering the King's Cellar at Paris*, by Johann Zoffany (Wadsworth Atheneum, Hartford), which appeared at the Royal Academy in 1795, may have partly prompted West to paint his contented, law-abiding Englishmen from a similar social stratum the following year. During 1796 he also painted the oil sketch of *Death on the Pale Horse* (cat. 38), a work not unaffected by recent developments across the channel.

Starting in Philadelphia as early as 1752, West did paint occasional landscapes throughout his career, but this type of subject also took on new importance for him in this late period, and most of his known or recorded landscapes date from between 1794 and 1812. They divide into two classes: views of actual scenery, generally on a modest scale, and more ambitious historical or imaginary landscapes. *The Sun Setting Behind a Group of Trees on the Banks of the Thames at Twickenham* (cat. 46), probably painted in 1799, is an example of the former. West certainly painted such works for relaxation, but his scenes of a tranquil English countryside also bear some of the same overtones of meaning as the peaceful and industrious populace in *A Drayman Drinking*. The twilight view of an anonymous stretch of river, which has been identified both as at Twickenham in the suburbs of London and as above Windsor further from the metropolis, shows how sensitively the artist could respond to natural effects when he allowed himself to do so. Nevertheless, if the view appears simple and straightforward, the effect of sunlight shining through trees and reflected on the water is more than simply naturalistic. In 1829 the painting was described as "wrought in the style and feeling of Rembrandt." It is one of three known pictures by West painted in the 1790's on the unusual support of slate, presumably as a technical experiment analogous to his experiments with the Venetian Secret.

Cicero Discovering the Tomb of Archimedes (cat. 43) of 1797, which has been discussed in conjunction with those experiments, was also West's most important historical landscape from the decade. It is based on an account in Cicero's *Tusculan Disputations*, written in 45 B.C., recalling the author's discovery of the tomb of the third-century B.C. mathematician Archimedes during a visit to Syracuse in Sicily thirty years previously. Cicero was able to identify it by remembering a description of a cylinder and sphere on top of the grave, which we see on the right of the painting. Behind Cicero pointing out his discovery to the locals, who had not known of the resting place of their most famous forebear, is an imaginary reconstruction of ancient Syracuse, with Mount Etna in the distance. The subject had been suggested to West by Sir George Beaumont, and it epitomizes the learned antiquarian and archaeological enthusiasms of the late eighteenth-century society in which West and Beaumont moved. The composition combining classical figures and invented landscape is strongly reminiscent of seventeenth-century historical landscapes by Nicolas Poussin.

West's activity as a landscape painter in the 1790's came just as the great efflorescence of English landscape was about to begin, when the careers of Thomas Girtin, John Constable, and J.M.W. Turner were starting to take form. *The Sun Setting Behind a Group of Trees* has affinities with landscapes by the former two, which, in the case of Constable, accompanied personal friendship. The "amiable president" took a benevolent interest in the younger artist, and among other pieces of advice, gave what Constable later said was the best lecture on chiaroscuro he ever heard: "Always remember, sir, that light and shadow *never stand still*."[11] Constable praised West's landscapes in a lecture given in 1833.[12] With Turner West was less friendly. In 1801 he spoke "in the highest manner" of Turner's works, but in 1805 he announced that Turner was "tending to imbecility," a progression in opinion from recognition of Turner's great abilities to censure of his originality.[13] Turner, nevertheless, did aspire to paint historical landscapes in the tradition of Poussin, adhering to the belief that their imaginative dimension gave to the lesser art of landscape some of the dignity of history painting. In England, the most significant eighteenth-century historical landscapes had been painted by Richard Wilson, but Wilson died in 1782, and works by West such as *Cicero Discovering the Tomb of Archimedes* exhibited in the 1790's were prominent links in the chain of tradition from Wilson to early paintings by Turner such as *The Goddess of Discord in the Garden of the Hesperides* (Tate Gallery) produced in the first decade of the next century.

Despite the role pictures of classical subjects played at the beginning of West's career, and despite our popular perception of him as a neoclassical artist, in the 1770's and 1780's he moved progressively away from Greece and Rome to specialize instead in subjects from English history and from the Bible. From 1782 to 1793 classical themes disappeared from his oeuvre, and when he turned back to them in the

Cat. 43. *Cicero Discovering the Tomb of Archimedes.* 1797
Oil on canvas. 49 x 71 in. (124.5 x 180.4 cm.)
Kennedy Galleries, Inc., New York

Cat. 67. *Thetis Bringing the Armour to Achilles.* 1805
Outline engraving by Henry Moses
Sheet: 15⅞ x 12¼ in. (403 x 311 mm.)
Friends Historical Library of Swarthmore College

1790's he often seems to have chosen them as neutral vehicles for technical exercises, which he did not want complicated by unfamiliar iconography or hortatory messages. West tried to discourage a patron from buying *A Bacchante* by disparaging it as "not of that class in composition by which my works are known; but one of those in the corse of my practice, I paint, to diversify my professional pursuits." *Bacchanti* were so frequently painted by so many artists— Reynolds, Romney, Hoppner, among others—that we must see the subject as a convenient non-subject, and, as we have seen from Farington's remark quoted above, West's prime concern in painting it was in achieving the luminosity of Titian. In that he succeeded well enough to create a ravishingly beautiful picture, but with none of the high-minded content of *Agrippina* and *Regulus* (cats. 11 and 12) of more than a quarter of a century before. *Cicero Discovering the Tomb of Archimedes* shows a less conventional subject and one, like those of *Agrippina* and *Regulus*, drawn from Roman history rather than the more standardized repertory of myth. Nevertheless, it differs from those works not only in its landscape dimension and its striking tonalities stemming

from the Venetian Secret, but also in its subject, which bears none of their allusions to sacrifice and duty. Rather than acting, suffering, or dying heroically, Cicero is an antique forerunner of the eighteenth-century gentlemen of the Society of Dilettanti, to which, not coincidentally, West was elected in 1792.

West's most important later painting of a classical subject was *Thetis Bringing the Armour to Achilles* of 1805, which has disappeared but is known via prints (cat. 67) and smaller variants of the original composition (cat. 49). The subject is from the nineteenth book of the *Iliad*. Achilles mourning the death of Patroclus, who has been slain by Hector, has withdrawn from the war against Troy. To persuade him to return to battle, his mother, Thetis, has had a new set of armor made by Hephaestus to replace Achilles's previous armor, which Patroclus had been wearing when he was killed. Achilles eventually does rededicate himself to the cause, but the image of a reluctant hero being bribed to pull himself together is the opposite of the forthright commitment to duty of Agrippina and Regulus. Additionally, the nude figures, the reduction of the composition to two main actors on a large scale (the original picture was eight feet high), the emphatic outline of Thetis's head, the generally linear design, and the elaboration of the armor Thetis is bringing and of other details all reflect a somewhat different purpose than that of making a convincing recreation of a historical event, which lay behind the earlier works. The composition of 1805 is more abstractly conceived, more decorative, more archaeological in its representation of the classical world.

There are several connected reasons for these changes. First was growing archaeological sophistication, owing to the explorations and publications sponsored by the Society of Dilettanti and other groups, which led to a growing concern with accurate classical detail in architecture and design. West painted the large *Thetis* for Thomas Hope, a leading figure in the Greek Revival of the early nineteenth-century and a scholar himself, who published a two-volume *Costume of the Ancients* in 1809 and other works devoted to antique furniture and decoration and modern equivalents in the same style. The engraver Henry Moses worked extensively for Hope, and his print of the *Thetis* (cat. 67) was the first plate in a book of outline engravings after West's compositions—the first monograph on the artist—which Moses published in 1811 with a dedication to Hope.

The archaeological style, which West followed and which is so sympathetically transcribed in Moses's engraving, traces back to the linearity and two-dimensionality of Greek vase paintings, but West (and Moses) learned it not directly from the Greeks, but from the immensely influential intermediary of outline engravings after designs by the sculptor John Flaxman, particularly those illustrating the *Iliad* and the *Odyssey* published in 1793 (Flaxman also drew a set of illustrations of Dante for Hope at the same time). West's *Thetis* has only slight compositional similarities to Flaxman's

Cat. 49. *Thetis Bringing the Armour to Achilles.* 1806(?)
Oil on canvas. 19½ x 26½ in. (49.5 x 67.3 cm.)
New Britain Museum of American Art:
Charles F. Smith Fund 42.10

Cat. 50. *Sketch for a Monument to Lord Nelson.* 1807
Oil on canvas. 39⅜ x 29¼ in. (100.1 x 74.3 cm.)
Yale Center for British Art, New Haven, Connecticut:
Paul Mellon Collection

illustration of the same subject, but it is linked to several related designs. He made an unusually large number of preparatory drawings for the work in which we can see him adapting and modifying Flaxman for his own purposes. In one respect, West also anticipated Flaxman. Book XVIII of the *Iliad* contains a long description of the emblems and scenes decorating Achilles's new shield, which West faithfully followed in minute detail. In Flaxman's outline illustration the shield is simpler, but in 1810 he began to design an actual shield as a tribute to the Duke of Wellington in which he also attempted to give form to Homer's description.

West's turn away from the style of *Agrippina* and the *Regulus* to the more abstract and archaeological manner of *Thetis* was also anticipated in France by Jacques-Louis David, who in the later 1790's disavowed his earlier paintings such as the *Oath of the Horatii* and the *Death of Socrates* to adopt the "Greek" style of his great *Sabines* completed in 1799 (Louvre), a work also significantly influenced by Flaxman's outlines. West saw the *Sabines* in Paris in 1802, and in that year's Salon he saw *Phaedra and Hippolytus* (also Louvre) painted by the younger Pierre-Narcisse Guérin, who "had carried the art further than David." What he saw must have encouraged him toward his own equivalent of the Greek style, which he only developed after the visit to Paris. The theatrically glowering Achilles, who does not have much precedent in West's own earlier painting, was probably inspired by the melodramatic Phaedra of Guérin, who stares out of the picture in a distraught way. West took theatricality further in the small later version (cat. 49) by adding Achilles's Myrmidons, whose fear of the new armor is described in the *Iliad*, and who serve as a chorus responding to the main event. This version, which probably was the version of the subject West exhibited at the Royal Academy in 1808, was also one of his last efforts in this manner. In 1808, his first exposure to the Parthenon sculptures, instead of encouraging the archaeological style, evidently made him realize how artificial it was. He told Lord Elgin in 1811 that if he had seen the sculptures sooner, "more character, and expression, and life would have pervaded all my humble attempts in Historical Painting," and the first picture he claimed was based on their principles was not classical but *Christ Healing the Sick.*[14]

In the spring of 1805, when West was painting Thetis arming her son to return to war, Britain was girding herself to withstand an expected invasion by Napoleon's armies following resumption of hostilities after the short-lived Peace of Amiens. That threat would be ended by the great naval victory over the French at Cape Trafalgar later in the year, in which the death of Lord Nelson in the hour of triumph echoed the death of Wolfe at Quebec in 1759. According to a story later told by West, Nelson, seated next to him at a dinner some time before Trafalgar, complimented him on *The Death of General Wolfe*, and asked why he had painted no more pictures like it. West's reply was, "Because, my

Lord, there are no more subjects . . . But . . . I fear your intrepidity will yet furnish me such another scene; and, if it should, I shall certainly avail myself of it." He did. Within three weeks of the news of Trafalgar reaching London, West and the engraver James Heath entered into a joint plan for a painting and an engraving after it (cat. 68), conceived as a companion to William Woollett's engraving after *The Death of General Wolfe* (cat. 61). West completed the picture in 1806 and exhibited it in his own studio with replicas of *The Death of General Wolfe* and *The Battle of La Hogue* displayed on either side (he had resigned the presidency of the Royal Academy the previous December, and 1806 was the one year between 1768 and 1820 he did not exhibit there). Heath completed his engraving five years later, and West re-exhibited the painting along with it at the Academy in 1811.

Like *The Death of General Wolfe*, *The Death of Lord Nelson* is notoriously inaccurate. After Nelson was wounded by a sniper's bullet, he was immediately taken below deck, and he died there, not on deck surrounded by all his officers and sailors. West's comments about "Epic representation" quoted on p. 54 were made in 1807 while justifying the liberties he had taken in *The Death of Lord Nelson*, and in 1811 the Royal Academy catalogue contained a long explanation of the picture in which the statement, "Mr. West conceiving that such an event demanded a composition every way appropriate to its dignity and high importance, formed it into an Epic Composition," was followed by an account of how he formed it—"he laid the heroic Nelson wounded on the quarterdeck . . ."—with no pretense of representing what had actually happened. Three years later the catalogue published to accompany *Christ Rejected* similarly asserted that that subject demanded an "Epic Composition," and, contemporary uniforms and portraits of participants notwithstanding, *The Death of Lord Nelson* and *Christ Rejected* have much in common. When spectators approached the former, West told Farington they were struck with reverence and instinctively pulled off their hats.

Cat. 50, dated 1807, is a sketch for a monument to Nelson combining architecture, sculpture, and painting. West did not win the commission for which the sketch was painted, and the actual monument in St. Paul's is by Flaxman, but West subsequently did adapt the central painted part of his proposed monument for an even grander sculptural ensemble on a pediment of one of the buildings of the Royal Naval Hospital at Greenwich. This pediment, which West modeled in artificial stone with the help of a sculptor named Joseph Panzetta, measures forty-five feet across and is his largest single work, although it remains one of his least known (it is in part of Greenwich closed to the public). The subject is an apotheosis of Nelson, in which a figure of Victory presents the body of the dead hero, handed up from the sea by Neptune, to Britannia shaded in grief. The freedom with which West reinvented Nelson's death as a public spectacle in the painting of 1806 has been carried a step further into

Cat. 44. *General Tadeusz Kosciuszko.* 1797
Oil on panel. 12⁵⁄₁₆ x 17⁵⁄₁₆ in. (31.3 x 44 cm.)
Allen Memorial Art Museum, Oberlin College:
R.T. Miller, Jr. Fund, 46.46

allegory. West had earlier depicted death allegorically in *The Apotheosis of Prince Alfred and Prince Octavius* of 1783 (see cat. 63). He also had seen, in the Salon of 1802 in Paris, the Ossianic *Apotheosis of the French Heroes* painted for Malmaison by Anne-Louis Girodet-Trioson, and could hardly have failed to remember it five years later. Nevertheless, the sketch was intended for a funerary monument, and it employs the traditional allegorical language of sculpted tombs. Victory accompanied by a putto carrying a crown of laurel, Britannia with her lion, Neptune with his trident (which West's Victory hands to Britannia) appear over and over on monuments to naval heroes. Comparable use of allegory was also not unknown in painting prior to 1770, and, in inveighing then against the use of modern dress, Reynolds probably had hoped West might depict the demise of Wolfe in a similarly traditional allegorical manner. West's success in presenting death in heroic terms while eschewing "classical fictions" so completely turned the tables that by 1807 allegorical painting was not only out of fashion, but looked upon as incomprehensibly bizarre. One critic, who found West's composition absurd, went on to declare, "The invisible world is not within the artist's province."

At the outset of his professional life, West supported himself by painting portraits. When he achieved recognition as a history painter, his output of portraits dropped off, and it virtually came to an end in the 1780's. In the 1790's and after 1800, as his work became more varied once again, he painted relatively few commissioned portraits, but several likenesses of himself (cat. 37), his family (cat. 40), friends (cat. 48), and at least one sitter (cat. 44) in response to his historical importance.

Tadeusz Kosciuszko (1746–1817), the subject of cat. 44 was a contemporary hero, a Pole who had served as a volunteer in the American revolutionary war, then returned to his homeland to fight for its freedom from Russian domination. In 1794 he was badly wounded and taken prisoner by the Russians. Released in 1796, he traveled via England to asylum in America. West together with John Trumbull, who had been a fellow officer with Kosciuszko in the American revolutionary army, visited him in his hotel in London in June 1797, and West presented to this modern Hector, who had devoted his recent life to a gallant fight in a losing cause, a drawing of *Hector Parting from Andromache*.[15] After Kosciuszko reached America, he in turn gave the drawing to Thomas Jefferson.

West painted the portrait of Kosciuszko from memory immediately after his visit and exhibited it at the Royal Academy in 1798. A Polish officer's cap in the foreground establishes the sitter's nationality. The sword next to it was presented to him by the English Whigs. A crutch and the bandage around his head remind us of the wounds from which he was suffering. The view of St. Paul's out the window, recalling the background of *A Drayman Drinking* of the previous year, places him in London. Papers scattered around the room are presumably landscape sketches, which West told Farington Kosciuszko drew as his principal amusement. West also told Farington that Kosciuszko had been lying on a couch during the visit, but his position in the painting, with his hand to head, suggests revery and melancholy as well as debilitated health. The small scale, more like that of a conversation piece than a formal portrait, reflects the fact that Kosciuszko did not pose for the picture; indeed, he was so shy of posing that another artist, Richard Cosway, was said to have sketched his portrait through a keyhole. The small scale also gives a sense of reportorial immediacy and candid informality and follows a tradition employed by Hogarth in depicting famous criminals and other newsworthy subjects. For West, the portrayal of such a real-life hero was partly journalistic and partly an extension of the role of portraits in his paintings of modern history, some of which such as the picture of the peace conference of 1782 (cat. 30) consisted of little more than portraiture.

The portrait of *Robert Fulton* of 1806 (cat. 48) was painted out of friendship and was given by the artist to the sitter. Fulton (1765–1815) came to London in 1786 to study painting under West. In the 1790's he abandoned art to pursue the scientific and technical interests that would lead to his achievement of fame as an inventor, and from 1797 to 1804 he lived in France. He returned to England as the inventor of a torpedo, which he hoped to sell to the British admiralty, and the view of an exploding ship in the background records a successful demonstration of his invention's effectiveness that had taken place in October 1805. Fulton went back to America a year later, taking with him not only this portrait, but also a self-portrait by West[16] and his large paintings from *King Lear* (see cat. 65) and *Hamlet*[17] painted originally for Boydell's Shakespeare Gallery, which Fulton bought when the gallery was dispersed in 1805. He placed them on loan in the new Pennsylvania Academy in Philadelphia, where they became the first major works by West exhibited publicly in America, a decade before the second *Christ Healing the Sick* reached the Pennsylvania Hospital. He also lobbied unsuccessfully in 1807 and 1810 to persuade the Pennsylvania Academy to purchase a collection of West's paintings as the nucleus of the first public collection in America. All this activity stemmed from long-standing familiarity with West's work, as Fulton was a native of Pennsylvania and grew up in Lancaster, where he was a protégé of the same William Henry for whom West had painted *The Death of Socrates* (cat. 2) in 1756.

West's affection for Fulton is evident from the portrait. Fulton is shown dressed in the height of up-to-date fashion, his hair in studied disarray, seated quietly, posing for his portrait. While his torpedo does its work in the background, he stares out at us with dark, burning eyes, through which we feel we look into his inner essence. Such intimate intensity had little antecedent in West's earlier portraiture and was alien to the more reserved conventions of eighteenth-century manners to which he generally adhered in art and life (compare his self-portrait of 1792, cat. 37). He may have been responding to the innate genius which Fulton unquestionably possessed, but he was also responding to new conceptions of portraiture coming into currency at the beginning of the nineteenth century and best represented by the work of Thomas Lawrence, who in 1820 would succeed West in the presidency of the Royal Academy. The inward focus of West's *Fulton* echoes Lawrence as much as the outward and active expression of the sitter's position in *General Monckton* (cat. 7) had echoed Reynolds forty-two years before.

The Bard (cat. 51) of 1809 belongs to the genre of literary painting, one to which, unlike portraiture, West had devoted himself increasingly in the 1770's, 1780's, and 1790's. He first painted subjects from English authors, Spenser and Shakespeare, in the 1770's. *Romeo and Juliet* of 1775–1778 (cat. 20) was his first Shakespearean picture and an early manifestation of the dramatically charged themes that artists found in English literature as rococo eroticism gave way to Romantic emotion. His most ambitious literary pictures were the *King Lear* and *Hamlet* for the Boydell Shakespeare Gallery, which he completed in 1788 and 1792 and retouched after they were purchased by Fulton in 1805. Since *The Bard* shows a protagonist reminiscent of Lear, it may have been partly inspired by renewed sight of the Boydell *King Lear*, but it illustrates an eighteenth-century poem, published in 1757, "The Bard" by Thomas Gray, which had widespread popularity among early nineteenth-century artists, including Blake, Turner, and John Martin. According to Welsh tradition, King Edward I of England, the thirteenth-century conqueror of Wales, had all the Welsh bards put to death in an effort to stamp out any vestiges of indigenous culture. In the poem, the last remaining bard, standing on Snowdon, the highest peak in Wales, calls down curses on the invading English, and then leaps to his death. The subject had an obvious appeal to landscape painters, who could set it in the wild sublimity of the Welsh mountains, but West, despite his late interest in landscape, shows only enough rocks and sky, plus an ominous flock of vultures in the background, to establish a high, wild, and evidently dangerous setting for a heroic, Michelangelesque figure, who fills the canvas. Contemporary discussions of Gray's poem, including a reference in Reynolds's final discourse, asserted that his bard was modeled on a sixteenth-century fresco of Moses by Parmigianino, and West's bard, while recalling both Parmigianino's and Michelangelo's *Moses*, was modeled on his own earlier *Moses* for the royal chapel at Windsor, transformed by the substitution of a lyre for the tables of the law.

The poem's popularity around 1800 was enhanced by its lament for Welsh independence at a time of growing awareness of national identity and of national movements throughout Europe to shake free from foreign domination. West had painted an oil sketch of the composition as early as 1778,[18] when the theme of defiance of English tyranny had clear relevance to the American colonies' struggle to free themselves from British rule. The opening line of the poem, "Ruin seize thee, ruthless King!", also reminds us of the current of anti-monarchical sentiment that had first appeared in his painting during the American Revolution. By 1809, the old bard's hostility to Edward I must have held additional personal meaning for the seventy-one-year-old painter, whose relations with his king were no longer what they had been and, with a regency of the Prince of Wales (a title created by Edward I to symbolize the subjugation of Wales) looming on the horizon, were only likely to get worse, as they did when he lost his income from the crown in the following year. The bard's raised arm might even be interpreted as the painter's own gesture of farewell. As things turned out, he had another productive decade of work ahead, during which fortune was to smile upon him (what evidently was his last painting is signed and dated October 10, 1819, his eighty-first birthday),[19] but *The Bard* does represent an ultimate point in West's artistic evolution, before he started to recycle earlier subjects and compositions in his late large religious works. It is manifestly a product of the Romantic era, of the century in which it was painted, and, if we think back to West's earliest pictures of literary subjects, to his *Angelica and Medoro* of 1763–1764 (cat. 6), we can see how far he had come. If the earlier work belongs to the world of Boucher, *The Bard* looks forward to Delacroix's *Greece on the Ruins of Missolonghi* (Musée des Beaux Arts, Bordeaux), painted in 1826 after Delacroix had seen West's works in London in 1825. Yet West's bard, a defiant old man about to take his own life, also had numerous antecedents in West's earlier work, starting with Socrates in cat. 2 of 1756. In West's long working life and his huge output, in which we can see an almost bewildering variety of interests and a stylistic evolution which associated him with almost every important artistic development for three quarters of a century, we can also see remarkable consistency and continuity from beginning to end.

Cat. 51. *The Bard.* 1809
Oil on canvas. 96 x 72 in. (243.9 x 183 cm.)
H. Shickman Gallery, New York

These notes supplement but do not repeat the references provided in the appropriate entries of *The Paintings of Benjamin West* by Helmut von Erffa and Allen Staley (Yale University Press, New Haven and London, 1986), where full documentation for every painting by West may be found.

NOTES TO CHAPTER 1:

1. Robert C. Alberts, *Benjamin West: A Biography* (Boston: Houghton Mifflin Company, 1978), pp. 8, 11.
2. Charles Henry Hart, "Benjamin West's Family. The American President of the Royal Academy of Arts Not a Quaker," *The Pennsylvania Magazine of History and Biography* 32 (1908):1–3; and Horace Mather Lippincott, "Benjamin West, 1757 C," *The General Magazine and Historical Chronicle* 47, no. 1 (August 1944):27.
3. Helmut von Erffa and Allen Staley, *The Paintings of Benjamin West* (New Haven and London: Yale University Press, 1986), p. 450.
4. John Galt, *The Life, Studies and Works of Benjamin West, Esq., President of the Royal Academy of London, Composed from Materials Furnished by Himself. . . Part II* (London: T. Cadell and W. Davies, Strand, 1820), p. vi.
5. Galt, 1820, p. vii.
6. John Galt, *The Life and Studies of Benjamin West, Esq., President of the Royal Academy of London, Prior to his Arrival in England, Compiled from Materials Furnished by Himself* (London: T. Cadell and W. Davies, Strand, 1816), pp. 18, 21.
7. David H. Dickason, "Benjamin West on William Williams: A Previously Unpublished Letter," *Winterthur Portfolio* 6 (1970):130.
8. Kenneth Garlick, Angus Macintyre, and Kathryn Cave, eds., *The Diary of Joseph Farington*, 26 vols. (New Haven and London: Yale University Press, 1978–1984), vol. 6, p. 2480.
9. Leigh Hunt, *The Autobiography of Leigh Hunt with Reminiscences of Friends and Contemporaries*, 2 vols. (New York: Harper & Brothers), 1850, pp. 148–149.
10. von Erffa/Staley, nos. 480 and 481.
11. Ann Uhry Abrams, "A New Light on Benjamin West's Pennsylvania Instruction," *Winterthur Portfolio* 6 (Winter 1982):243–257.
12. von Erffa/Staley, nos. 667 and 668.
13. William Carey, "Memoirs of Benjamin West, Esq.," *New Monthly Magazine* 13 (May 1820):515.
14. "Royal Academy," *True Briton*, December 11, 1794.
15. Galt, 1816, p. 122.
16. von Erffa/Staley, nos. 504–521.
17. von Erffa/Staley, no. 582.
18. von Erffa/Staley, no. 195.
19. E.P. Richardson, "West's Voyage to Italy, 1760, and William Allen," *The Pennsylvania Magazine of History and Biography* 102 (1978):23. Rutherford's letters to Shippen are in the American Philosophical Society in Philadelphia.
20. von Erffa/Staley, no. 188.
21. von Erffa/Staley, no. 700.
22. See Dorinda Evans, *Benjamin West and His American Students* (exhibition catalogue), Washington, D.C., Smithsonian Institution Press, 1980.
23. Ruth S. Kraemer, *Drawings by Benjamin West and his son Raphael Lamar West* (exhibition catalogue), New York, The Pierpont Morgan Library, 1975, p. 87.
24. Nicholas Penny, ed., *Reynolds* (exhibition catalogue), London, Royal Academy of Arts, 1986, nos. 113 and 116.
25. Galt, 1820, pp. 189–190.
26. Hunt, p. 148.

NOTES TO CHAPTER 2:

1. von Erffa/Staley, nos. 692, 693.
2. See p. 14 of this text.
3. R. Peter Mooz, "Robert Feke: The Philadelphia Story," in Ian M.G. Quimby, ed., *American Painting to 1776: A Reappraisal* (Winterthur, Delaware: The Henry Francis du Pont Winterthur Museum, 1971), pp. 181–216.
4. Ann Uhry Abrams, *The Valiant Hero: Benjamin West and Grand-Style History Painting* (Washington, D.C.: Smithsonian Institution Press, 1985), pp. 61–62.
5. Albert Frank Gegenheimer, *Thomas Godfrey: Protégé of William Smith* (Philadelphia: University of Pennsylvania, 1943), p. 12.
6. Richard H. Saunders and Ellen G. Miles, *American Colonial Portraits: 1700–1776* (exhibition catalogue), National Portrait Gallery, Washington, D.C., 1987, no. 65; and "Letter from Benjamin West," *Journal of the Archives of American Art* 4 (January 1964):11.
7. Illustrated in von Erffa/Staley, p. 6.
8. Galt, 1816, pp. 119–122; and von Erffa/Staley, p. 689.
9. von Erffa/Staley, nos. 582, 658, and 730.
10. von Erffa/Staley, nos. 581, 583, 584, and 700.
11. von Erffa/Staley, no. 661.
12. von Erffa/Staley, nos. 659, 660, and 662.
13. Penny, nos. 19 and 26.
14. Lorenz Eitner, ed., *Neoclassicism and Romanticism 1750–1850*, vol. 1, *Enlightenment/Revolution*, Sources & Documents in the History of Art Series, edited by H.W. Janson (Englewood Cliffs, New Jersey: Prentice-Hall, Inc., 1970), pp. 6–7; quoted from the translation by Henry Fuseli (London, 1765).
15. Galt, 1816, pp. 103–106.
16. von Erffa/Staley, no. 520.
17. von Erffa/Staley, no. 504.
18. von Erffa/Staley, nos. 226, 227, 229, and 230.
19. von Erffa/Staley, no. 243.

NOTES TO CHAPTER 3:

1. "Letter from Benjamin West," *Journal of the Archives of American Art* 4 (January 1964):12.
2. von Erffa/Staley, no. 141.
3. Anthony M. Clark, *Pompeo Batoni* (New York: New York University Press, 1985), nos. 67, 123, 173, and 288.
4. Galt, 1816, p. 106.
5. Eitner, pp. 31–32.
6. von Erffa/Staley, nos. 278, 292, 312, and 321.
7. von Erffa/Staley, nos. 223, 224, and 294.
8. von Erffa/Staley, no. 591.
9. Francis Haskell and Nicholas Penny, *Taste and the Antique: The Lure of Classical Sculpture 1500–1900* (New Haven and London: Yale University Press, 1981), pp. 141–142.

NOTES TO CHAPTER 4:

1. von Erffa/Staley, nos. 96 and 97.
2. *Farington Diary*, p. 3064.
3. von Erffa/Staley, no. 94.
4. Unlocated, but known from an undated engraving by Juste Chevillet (1729–1790).
5. Ann Uhry Abrams, *The Valiant Hero*, pp. 192–195; see also the same author's "Benjamin West's Documentation of Colonial History: William Penn's Treaty with the Indians," *Art Bulletin* 64 (March 1982):59–75.
6. von Erffa/Staley, no. 584.
7. von Erffa/Staley, nos. 83 and 88.

NOTES TO CHAPTER 5:

1. Galt, 1820, pp. 32–33.
2. Francis Russell, "King George III's picture hang at Buckingham House," *Burlington Magazine* 129 (August 1987):524–531.
3. H.T. Watlington, "The Incomplete Story of John Green: Artist and Judge," *Bermuda Historical Quarterly* 6 (April–June 1949):67.
4. von Erffa/Staley, no. 17.
5. von Erffa/Staley, nos. 2 and 32.
6. von Erffa/Staley, nos. 58, 67, and 74.
7. Galt, 1820, p. 72.
8. von Erffa/Staley, no. 58. For the arrangement of the room, see Wendy Greathouse, "Benjamin West and Edward III: A Neoclassical Painter and Medieval History," *Art History* 8 (June 1985):178–191, fig. 27.
9. Galt, 1820, p. 52.
10. von Erffa/Staley, pp. 577–581.
11. von Erffa/Staley, nos. 286 and 258.
12. von Erffa/Staley, nos. 298, 306, 309, 356, and 360.
13. von Erffa/Staley, nos. 437, 438, and 439.
14. von Erffa/Staley, nos. 562, 564, and 568.
15. *Farington Diary*, vol. 1, p. 99.
16. *Farington Diary*, vol. 1, p. 270.
17. von Erffa/Staley, nos. 210 and 211.

NOTES TO CHAPTER 6:

1. Morton D. Paley, *The Apocalyptic Sublime* (New Haven and London: Yale University Press, 1986), p. 1.
2. von Erffa/Staley, nos. 276 and 288.
3. Alberts, p. 122.
4. von Erffa/Staley, no. 388.
5. von Erffa/Staley, no. 685.
6. See p. 57 of this text.
7. von Erffa/Staley, no. 402.
8. von Erffa/Staley, no. 401.
9. von Erffa/Staley, no. 415.
10. *Farington Diary*, vol. 3, p. 912.
11. Charlotte Lansdown, ed., *Recollections of the Late William Beckford, of Fonthill, Wilts; and Lansdown, Bath* (Privately printed, 1893), p. 13.
12. Nancy L. Pressly, *Revealed Religion: Benjamin West's Commissions for Windsor Castle and Fonthill Abbey* (exhibition catalogue), San Antonio Museum of Art, 1983, p. 64.
13. Draper Hill, *Mr. Gillray: The Caricaturist* (London: The Phaidon Press, 1965), pl. 51.
14. Louvre, R.F. 5 278. See Maurice Sérullaz, *Mémorial de l'exposition Eugène Delacroix* (exhibition catalogue), Musées Nationaux, Paris, 1963, no. 104, ill.
15. See the *Apotheosis of the French Heroes* (Musée National du Château, Rueil-Malmaison) by Girodet and *The Battle of Nazareth* (Musée des Beaux Arts, Nantes) by Gros, both reproduced and discussed in Frederick J. Cummings, Pierre Rosenberg, and Robert Rosenblum's *French Painting 1774–1830: The Age of Revolution* (exhibition catalogue), Detroit Institute of Arts and The Metropolitan Museum of Art, 1975, nos. 80 and 88.
16. *Farington Diary*, vol. 6, p. 1853.
17. Hunt, pp. 149–150; *Farington Diary*, vol. 8, p. 2908. For George III's growing hostility to West after 1802, see, for example, *Farington Diary*, vol. 6, pp. 2410, 2470.

NOTES TO CHAPTER 7:

1. von Erffa/Staley, no. 135.
2. von Erffa/Staley, no. 353.
3. von Erffa/Staley, no. 401.
4. von Erffa/Staley, no. 338.
5. *Farington Diary*, vol. 13, p. 4593.
6. von Erffa/Staley, no. 498.
7. In addition to the references cited in the pertinent entries of von Erffa/Staley (nos. 22, 133, 356, and 543), see William L. Pressly, ed., "Facts and Recollections of the XVIIIth Century in a Memoir of John Francis Rigaud, Esq., R.A.," *Walpole Society* 50 (1984):99–103.
8. W. Buchanan, *Memoirs of Painting*, 2 vols. (London: R. Ackerman, 1824), vol. 1, p. 9.
9. *Farington Diary*, vol. 2, p. 590; and John Landseer, *A Descriptive, Explanatory, and Critical Catalogue of Fifty of the Earliest Pictures Contained in the National Gallery of Great Britain* (London, 1834), p. 111.
10. Stephen Deuchar, *Paintings, Politics and Porter: Samuel Whitbread II (1764–1815) and British Art* (exhibition catalogue), Museum of London, 1984, nos. 5, 6, 20, and 21.
11. C.R. Leslie, *Memoirs of the Life of John Constable* (1843; reprint ed., London: The Phaidon Press, 1951), p. 14.
12. Leslie, p. 322.
13. *Farington Diary*, vol. 4, p. 1539, and vol. 7, p. 2555.
14. [William Richard Hamilton], *Memorandum on the Subject of the Earl of Elgin's Pursuits in Greece* (London: W. Miller, 1811), pp. 53–55.
15. von Erffa/Staley, no. 165.
16. von Erffa/Staley, no. 530.
17. von Erffa/Staley, no. 207.
18. von Erffa/Staley, no. 199.
19. von Erffa/Staley, no. 124.

I wish to record my indebtedness to the late Professor Helmut von Erffa who devoted his life to the study of Benjamin West. I am also grateful for the enlightened and generous support of my subsequent attention to West provided by Robert L. McNeil, Jr. and The Barra Foundation.

A.S.

Cat. 58. *The Death of Epaminondas.* 1774
Mezzotint by Valentine Green
Sheet: 25½ x 20⁹⁄₁₆ in. (648 x 523 mm.)
The Baltimore Museum of Art: Garrett Collection
(BMA 1946.112.10508)

Contents of the Exhibition

Works are catalogued in chronological order and titles are assigned by the owners. Dimensions are cited in inches and centimeters for paintings, in inches and millimeters for prints, height preceding width. Dates that appear on works are cited without parentheses; dates ascribed on either documentary or stylistic basis are cited in parentheses. The catalogue number from the 1986 definitive monograph, *The Paintings of Benjamin West*, co-authored by the late Helmut von Erffa and Allen Staley and published by Yale University Press, is cited in brackets. The reader will find detailed information for each painting listed in the von Erffa/Staley catalogue.

PAINTINGS

1. *George Ross*. (ca. 1755–1756). Oil on canvas. 42½ x 33½ in. (108 x 85.1 cm.). College Collections, Gift of Mrs. George Ross Eshleman, Franklin and Marshall College, Lancaster, Pennsylvania. Ill. p. 28 [691].

2. *The Death of Socrates*. (ca. 1756). Oil on canvas. 34 x 41 in. (86.4 x 104.2 cm.). Private Collection. Ill. p. 15 [4].

3. *Elizabeth Peel*. (ca. 1757–1758). Oil on canvas. 47⅛ x 34⅜ in. (119.7 x 87.3 cm.). Pennsylvania Academy of the Fine Arts, Philadelphia: Gift of John Frederick Lewis. Ill. p. 30 [681].

4. *Anne, Countess of Northampton, and Her Daughter, Lady Elizabeth Compton*. 1762. Oil on canvas. 51¼ x 41½ in. (130.2 x 105.5 cm.). Bass Museum of Art: Gift of John and Johanna Bass, 63.32. Ill. p. 17 [676].

5. *The Cricketers*. (1763?). Oil on canvas. 40 x 50 in. (101.6 x 127 cm.). Private Collection. Ill. p. 26 [726].

6. *Angelica and Medoro*. (ca. 1763–1764). Oil on canvas. 36¼ x 28¼ in. (92.1 x 71.8 cm.). University Art Gallery, State University of New York at Binghamton. Ill. p. 35 [188].

7. *Lieutenant General the Honorable Robert Monckton*. (ca. 1764). Oil on canvas. 94½ x 68⅜ in. (240.1 x 173.7 cm.). The Descendants of the 8th Viscount Galway. Ill. p. 32 [665].

8. *Jacob Blessing the Sons of Joseph*. 1766. Oil on canvas. 40¹⁄₁₆ x 51 in. (101.8 x 129.6 cm.). Allen Memorial Art Museum, Oberlin College: R. T. Miller, Jr. Fund, 61.70. Ill. p. 20 [250].

9. *Robert Auriol Hay Drummond, 9th Earl of Kinnoull, and His Brother, Thomas Drummond*. 1767. Oil on canvas. 94¾ x 58½ in. (240.8 x 148.6 cm.). Addison Gallery of American Art, Phillips Academy, Andover, Massachusetts. Ill. p. 40 [608].

10. *Venus Lamenting the Death of Adonis*. 1768/1819. Oil on canvas. 62 x 68 in. (157.5 x 172.8 cm.). The Carnegie Museum of Art, Pittsburgh: Purchase, 1911. Ill. p. 45 [116].

11. *Agrippina Landing at Brundisium with the Ashes of Germanicus*. 1768. Oil on canvas. 64½ x 94½ in. (164 x 240.1 cm.). Yale University Art Gallery, Gift of Louis M. Rabinowitz. Ill. p. 42 [33].

12. *The Departure of Regulus from Rome*. 1769. Oil on canvas. 88½ x 120 in. (224.9 x 304.9 cm.). Her Majesty Queen Elizabeth II. Ill. p. 43 [10].

13. *The Death of General Wolfe*. 1770. Oil on canvas. 60 x 84 in. (152.5 x 213.4 cm.). National Gallery of Canada, Ottawa: Deposited by Canadian War Memorials Fund, 1921. Ill. p. 53 [93].

14. *Mrs. West with Raphael West*. (ca. 1770). Oil on canvas. 36 in. diameter (91.5 cm. diameter). Marriner S. Eccles Foundation for the Marriner S. Eccles Masterwork Collection, Utah Museum of Fine Arts, Salt Lake City. Ill. p. 21 [538].

15. *Penn's Treaty with the Indians*. 1771–(1772). Oil on canvas. 75½ x 107¾ in. (191.8 x 273.8 cm.). Pennsylvania Academy of the Fine Arts, Philadelphia: Gift of Mrs. Sarah Harrison (The Joseph Harrison, Jr. Collection). Ill. p. 60 [85].

16. *The Death of the Chevalier Bayard.* 1772. Oil on canvas. 87¼ x 70½ in. (221.7 x 179.1 cm.). Her Majesty Queen Elizabeth II. Ill. p. 55 [77].

17. *The West Family.* (ca. 1772). Oil on canvas. 20½ x 26¼ in. (52.1 x 66.7 cm.). Yale Center for British Art, New Haven, Connecticut: Paul Mellon Collection. Ill. p. 19 [546].

18. *Chryses, the Priest of Apollo, on the Seashore, Invoking His God to Avenge the Injuries Done Him by Agamemnon.* 1773. Oil on canvas. 50 x 40 in. (127.1 x 101.6 cm.). Mount Holyoke College Art Museum, South Hadley, Massachusetts: The Warbeke Museum Fund, 1982. Ill. p. 47 [159].

19. *Cymon and Iphigenia.* 1773. Oil on canvas. 49 x 63 in. (124.5 x 160.1 cm.). Los Angeles County Museum of Art: Museum Purchase with Funds Provided by Mr. and Mrs. Reese Llewellyn Milner, Mr. and Mrs. Byron E. Vandergrift, George C. Zachary, Jo Ann and Julian Ganz, Jr., and Joseph T. Mendelson. Ill. p. 50 [228].

20. *Romeo and Juliet.* (ca. 1775)–1778. Oil on canvas. 44½ x 59 in. (113.1 x 150 cm.). New Orleans Museum of Art: Museum Purchase through Women's Volunteer Committee Funds. Ill. p. 39 [217].

21. *The Battle of La Hogue.* (ca. 1775–1780). Oil on canvas. 60⅛ x 84⅜ in. (152.8 x 214.4 cm.). National Gallery of Art, Washington, D.C.: Andrew W. Mellon Fund 1959.8.1. Ill. p. 61 [90].

22. *St. Michael and Satan.* 1776. Oil on paper mounted on canvas. 45 x 28½ in. (114.3 x 72.4 cm.). Collection of James Ricau on extended loan to The Brooklyn Museum. Ill. p. 66 [407].

23. *Six Children of George III.* 1776. Oil on canvas. 66¼ x 71 in. (168.3 x 180.4 cm.). Her Majesty Queen Elizabeth II. Ill. p. 77 [570].

24. *Self-Portrait.* (ca. 1776). Oil on canvas. 30¼ x 25⅛ in. (76.9 x 63.8 cm.). The Baltimore Museum of Art: Gift of Dr. Morton K. Blaustein, Barbara B. Hirschhorn, and Elizabeth B. Roswell, in Memory of Jacob and Hilda K. Blaustein (BMA 1981.73). Ill. cover and p. 12 (detail) [526].

25. *Saul and the Witch of Endor.* 1777. Oil on canvas. 20½ x 27 in. (52.1 x 68.6 cm.). Wadsworth Atheneum, Hartford: Bequest of Mrs. Clara Hinton Gould. Ill. p. 86 [275].

26. *Mr. and Mrs. John Custance.* 1778. Oil on canvas. 59 x 83 in. (150 x 210.9 cm.). The Nelson-Atkins Museum of Art, Kansas City, Missouri (Nelson Fund). Ill. p. 49 [607].

27. *The Death of the Earl of Chatham.* (ca. 1778/1786). Oil on canvas. 28 x 35¾ in. (71.1 x 90.8 cm.). Kimbell Art Museum, Fort Worth, Texas. Ill. p. 56 [104].

28. *Queen Charlotte.* 1779. Oil on canvas. 100½ x 72 in. (255.4 x 183 cm.). Her Majesty Queen Elizabeth II. Ill. p. 79 [556].

29. *General Monk Receiving Charles II on the Beaches of Dover.* 1782. Oil on canvas. 60 x 85 in. (152.5 x 216 cm.). Layton Art Collection, Milwaukee Art Museum. Ill. p. 63 [84].

30. *American Commissioners of the Preliminary Peace Negotiations with Great Britain.* (ca. 1783). Oil on canvas. 28½ x 36½ in. (72.5 x 92.5 cm.). Courtesy of the Henry Francis du Pont Winterthur Museum, Winterthur, Delaware. Ill. p. 58 [105].

31. *Isaiah's Lips Anointed with Fire.* (ca. 1784). Oil on canvas. 150 x 61 in. (381.1 x 155 cm.). Bob Jones University, Greenville, South Carolina. Ill. p. 72 [283].

32. *Edward III Crossing the Somme.* 1788. Oil on canvas. 54 x 59 in. (137.2 x 149.9 cm.). Her Majesty Queen Elizabeth II. Ill. p. 69 [56].

33. *Edward the Black Prince, Receiving John, King of France, Prisoner, after the Battle of Poitiers.* (ca. 1788). Oil on canvas. 16½ x 25½ in. (41.9 x 64.8 cm.). Collection George E. Doty, New York. Ill. p. 70 [75].

34. *Agriculture (Husbandry Aided by Arts and Commerce).* 1789. Oil on paper mounted on panel. 20 x 24 in. (50.8 x 61 cm.), oval. Mint Museum, Charlotte, North Carolina: Gift of the Woman's Auxiliary. Ill. p. 74 [436].

35. *Genius Calling Forth the Fine Arts to Adorn Manufactures and Commerce.* 1789. Oil on paper. 19½ x 24¾ in. (49.5 x 62.9 cm.). The Fine Arts Museums of San Francisco, Gift of Mr. and Mrs. John D. Rockefeller 3rd. Ill. p. 75 [435].

36. *His Majesty George III Resuming Power in 1789.* (ca. 1789). Oil on canvas. 20⁷⁄₁₆ x 30¼ in. (51.9 x 76.9 cm.). Hirschl & Adler Galleries, Inc., New York. Ill. p. 81 [107].

37. *Self-Portrait.* (1792). Oil on panel. 40 x 52 in. (101.6 x 132.1 cm.). The Royal Academy of Arts, London. Ill. pp. 2 (detail) and 24 [527].

38. *Death on the Pale Horse.* 1796. Oil on canvas. 23½ x 50½ in. (59.7 x 128.3 cm.). The Detroit Institute of Arts: Founders Society Purchase, Robert H. Tannahill Foundation Fund. Ill. p. 84 [403].

39. *A Drayman Drinking.* 1796. Oil on canvas. 15½ x 21 in. (39.4 x 53.4 cm.). Collection Dr. and Mrs. Henry C. Landon III. Ill. p. 98 [443].

40. *Raphael and Benjamin West, Sons of the Artist.* (1796). Oil on canvas. 35¼ x 28¼ in. (89.6 x 71.8 cm.). The Nelson-Atkins Museum of Art, Kansas City, Missouri (Gift of the Laura Nelson Kirkwood Residuary Trust). Ill. p. 22 [543].

41. *A Bacchante*. 1797. Oil on canvas. 50 x 40 in. (127.1 x 101.6 cm.). Collection Muriel and Philip Berman, Allentown, Pennsylvania. Ill. p. 97 [123].

42. *The Beast Riseth Out of the Sea*. 1797. Oil on panel. 31½ x 21½ in. (80 x 54.6 cm.). Collection Thomas and Margaret McCormick, Norton, Massachusetts. Ill. p. 90 [409].

43. *Cicero Discovering the Tomb of Archimedes*. 1797. Oil on canvas. 49 x 71 in. (124.5 x 180.4 cm.). Kennedy Galleries, Inc., New York. Ill. p. 101 [22].

44. *General Tadeusz Kosciuszko*. 1797. Oil on panel. 12⁵⁄₁₆ x 17⁵⁄₁₆ in. (31.3 x 44 cm.). Allen Memorial Art Museum, Oberlin College: R.T. Miller, Jr. Fund, 46.46. Ill. p. 106 [650].

45. *St. Michael and the Dragon*. (ca. 1797). Oil on canvas. 50½ x 23⁹⁄₁₆ in. (128.3 x 59.9 cm.). The Toledo Museum of Art: Museum Purchase Fund. Ill. p. 88 [408].

46. *The Sun Setting Behind a Group of Trees on the Banks of the Thames at Twickenham*. 1799(?). Oil on slate. 12 x 17 in. (30.5 x 43.2 cm.). The Charles P. Russell Collection of Deerfield Academy, Deerfield, Massachusetts. Ill. p. 99 [470].

47. *Noah Sacrificing*. (ca. 1801). Oil on canvas. 72 x 138 in. (183 x 350.7 cm.). Collection San Antonio Museum Association, San Antonio, Texas. Ill. p. 73 [236].

48. *Robert Fulton*. 1806. Oil on canvas. 35½ x 27½ in. (90.2 x 69.9 cm.). New York State Historical Association, Cooperstown. Ill. p. 93 [620].

49. *Thetis Bringing the Armour to Achilles*. 1806(?). Oil on canvas. 19½ x 26½ in. (49.5 x 67.3 cm.). New Britain Museum of American Art: Charles F. Smith Fund 42.10. Ill. p. 103 [175].

50. *Sketch for a Monument to Lord Nelson*. 1807. Oil on canvas. 39⅜ x 29¼ in. (100.1 x 74.3 cm.). Yale Center for British Art, New Haven, Connecticut: Paul Mellon Collection. Ill. p. 104 [110].

51. *The Bard*. 1809. Oil on canvas. 96 x 72 in. (243.9 x 183 cm.). H. Shickman Gallery, New York. Ill. p. 109 [198].

52. *Study for Christ Rejected*. 1811. Oil on paper mounted on panel. 30¼ x 42¼ in. (76.9 x 107.4 cm.). Memorial Art Gallery of the University of Rochester: Marion Stratton Gould Fund. Ill. p. 95 [354].

PRINTS

Where a print is based on a West painting, the von Erffa/Staley catalogue number for the original work is given in brackets.

53. *Praevalebit Aequior*. (ca. 1757). Attributed to Benjamin West. Published by Provost Smith as cover illustration of any issue of *The American Magazine and Monthly*

Chronicle for the British Colonies, Philadelphia, 1757–1758. Sheet: 8 x 5 in. (203 x 127 mm.). Rare Books Room, Library of Congress, Washington, D.C. Ill. p. 29.

54. *Savage Warrior Taking Leave of His Family*. 1763. Engraving by Francesco Bartolozzi (Italian, ca. 1725–1815). Published as frontispiece in *Storia degli stabilimenti europei in America*, Venice, 1763 (anonymous Italian translation of Edmund Burke's *An Account of the European Settlements in America*, London, 1757). Sheet: 5¹³⁄₁₆ x 3¹¹⁄₁₆ in. (147 x 94 mm.). Rare Book and Manuscript Library, Columbia University. Ill. p. 33 [see 452].

55. *Indians Giving a Talk to Colonel Bouquet in a Conference at a Council Fire, near his Camp on the Banks of Muskingum in North America in Oct. 1764*. (1766). Engraving by Charles Grignion (French, 1716–1810). In William Smith's *Account of the Expedition Against the Ohio Indians*, 2nd ed., 1766, opposite page 14. Sheet: 10 x 8½ in. (254 x 216 mm.). Rare Books Room, Library of Congress, Washington, D.C. Ill. p. 34.

Cat. 57.

Cat. 59.

Cat. 61.

56. *Venus Relating to Adonis the Story of Hippomenes and Atalanta*. 1769. Engraving in reverse by John Hall (English, 1739–1797). Published September 1, 1769 by J. Boydell. Sheet: 18 x 22¾ in. (457 x 578 mm.). The Baltimore Museum of Art: Garrett Collection (BMA 1946.112.15443). Ill. p. 37 [112].

57. *Mrs. West with Raphael West*. (before 1770). Mezzotint by Valentine Green (English, 1739–1813). Published July 10, 1770 by Robert Sayer. Sheet: 16³⁄₁₆ x 12¼ in. (411 x 311 mm.). The Baltimore Museum of Art: Garrett Collection (BMA 1946.112.10159). Ill. p. 115 [535].

58. *The Death of Epaminondas*. 1774. Mezzotint by Valentine Green. Published February 21, 1774 by J. Boydell. Sheet: 25½ x 20⁹⁄₁₆ in. (648 x 523 mm.). The Baltimore Museum of Art: Garrett Collection (BMA 1946.112.10508). Ill. p. 112 [5].

59. *Penn's Treaty with the Indians*. 1775. Engraving by John Hall. Published June 12, 1775 by John Boydell. Sheet: 19¼ x 24¾ in. (489 x 629 mm.). The Baltimore Museum of Art: Garrett Collection (BMA 1946.112.15442). Ill. p. 116 [85].

60. *Self-Portrait with Raphael West*. 1775. Mezzotint by Valentine Green. Published February 13, 1775 by Valentine Green. Sheet: 15⁷⁄₁₆ x 11 in. (392 x 280 mm.). The Baltimore Museum of Art: Garrett Collection (BMA 1946.112.10158). Ill. p. 23 [533].

61. *The Death of General Wolfe*. 1776. Engraving by William Woollett (English, 1735–1785). Published January 1, 1776 by Woollett, Boydell, and Ryland. Sheet: 18¹⁵⁄₁₆ x 23¼ in. (481 x 591 mm.). The Metropolitan Museum of Art: Gift of Georgiana W. Sargent in memory of John Osborne Sargent, 1924. Ill. p. 116 [93].

62. *George, Prince of Wales, with Prince Frederick*. 1779. Mezzotint by Valentine Green. Published November 4, 1779 by John Boydell. Sheet: 25⁹⁄₁₆ x 17⁵⁄₁₆ in. (650 x 440 mm.). The Baltimore Museum of Art: Garrett Collection (BMA 1946.112.10498). Ill. p. 78 [564].

63. *The Apotheosis of Prince Alfred and Prince Octavius*. 1786. Engraving by Robert Strange (English, 1721–1792). Published 1786 by Robert Strange. Sheet: 24½ x 17¾ in. (623 x 451 mm.). The Metropolitan Museum of Art: Gift of Georgiana W. Sargent in memory of John Osborne Sargent, 1924. Ill. p. 80 [575].

64. *St. Paul Shaking the Viper from his Hand After the Shipwreck*. 1791. Engraving by Francesco Bartolozzi. Published January 1, 1791 by Benjamin West and J.

Cat. 68.

116

Barney. Sheet: 29⅛ x 17¹⁵⁄₁₆ in. (740 x 456 mm.). The Baltimore Museum of Art: Garrett Collection (BMA 1946.112.14663). Ill. p. 71 [397].

65. *King Lear: Act III, Scene IV (King Lear in the Storm)*. 1793. Engraving by William Sharp (English, 1749–1824). Published March 26, 1793 by John and Josiah Boydell. Sheet: 21¹⁄₁₆ x 27⁹⁄₁₆ in. (535 x 700 mm.). The Baltimore Museum of Art: Garrett Collection (BMA 1946.112.8036). Ill. p. 82 [210].

66. *Angel of the Resurrection*. 1801. Lithograph by Benjamin West. Published by P. André, ed., *Specimens of Polyautography Consisting of Impressions Taken from Original Drawings made on stone purposely for this work*, London, 1803. 12⁷⁄₁₆ x 9 in. (316 x 229 mm.). National Gallery of Art, Washington: Rosenwald Collection, 1947.7.135. Ill. p. 96.

67. *Thetis Bringing the Armour to Achilles*. 1805. Outline engraving by Henry Moses (English, ca. 1782–1870). Published May 1, 1811. Sheet: 15⅞ x 12¼ in. (403 x 311 mm.). Friends Historical Library of Swarthmore College. Ill. p. 102 [170].

68. *The Death of Lord Nelson*. 1811. Engraving by James Heath (English, 1757–1834). Published May 1, 1811 by Benjamin West and James Heath. Sheet: 19¾ x 24¹⁵⁄₁₆ in. (502 x 634 mm.). The Metropolitan Museum of Art: Gift of Georgiana W. Sargent in memory of John Osborne Sargent, 1924. Ill. p. 116 [108].

69. *Christ Healing the Sick in the Temple*. 1822. Engraving by Charles Heath (English, 1785–1848). Published May 15, 1822 by G. & W. Nicol. Sheet: 22⁹⁄₁₆ x 30⅜ in. (573 x 772 mm.). The Baltimore Museum of Art: Garrett Collection (BMA 1946.112.15455). Ill. p. 117 [336].

Cat. 69.

SELECTED BIBLIOGRAPHY

Ann Uhry Abrams. *The Valiant Hero: Benjamin West and Grand-Style History Painting*. Washington, D.C.: Smithsonian Institution Press, 1985.

Robert C. Alberts. *Benjamin West: A Biography*. Boston: Houghton Mifflin Company, 1978.

Frederick J. Cummings, Robert Rosenblum, and Allen Staley. *Romantic Art in Britain: Paintings and Drawings 1760–1860* (exhibition catalogue). Detroit Institute of Arts and Philadelphia Museum of Art, 1968.

Stephen Deuchar. *Paintings, Politics and Porter: Samuel Whitbread and British Art* (exhibition catalogue). Museum of London, 1984.

Helmut von Erffa and Allen Staley. *The Paintings of Benjamin West*. New Haven and London: Yale University Press, 1986.

Dorinda Evans. *Benjamin West and His American Students* (exhibition catalogue). National Portrait Gallery, Washington, D.C., 1980.

James Thomas Flexner. "Benjamin West's American Neo-Classicism." *The New-York Historical Society Quarterly* 36 (1952):5–33.

Franziska Forster-Hahn. "The Source of True Taste: Benjamin West's Instructions to a Young Painter for His Studies in Italy." *Journal of the Warburg and Courtauld Institutes* 30 (1967):367–382.

John Galt. *The Life and Studies of Benjamin West, Esq., President of the Royal Academy of London, Prior to his Arrival in England, Compiled from Materials Furnished by Himself*. London: T. Cadell and W. Davies, Strand, 1816.

John Galt. *The Life, Studies and Works of Benjamin West, Esq., President of the Royal Academy of London, Composed from Materials Furnished by Himself . . . Part II*. London: T. Cadell and W. Davies, Strand, 1820.

Kenneth Garlick, Angus Macintyre, and Kathryn Cave, eds. *The Diary of Joseph Farington*. 26 vols. New Haven and London: Yale University Press, 1978–1984.

Wendy Greathouse. "Benjamin West and Edward III: A Neoclassical Painter and Medieval History." *Art History* 8 (June 1985):178–191.

Ruth S. Kraemer. *Drawings by Benjamin West and his son Raphael Lamar West* (exhibition catalogue). The Pierpont Morgan Library, New York, 1975.

Arthur S. Marks. "Benjamin West and the American Revolution." *The American Art Journal* 6 (November 1974):15–35.

Jerry D. Meyer. "Benjamin West's Chapel of Revealed Religion: A Study in Eighteenth-Century Protestant Religious Art." *Art Bulletin* 62 (1975):247–265.

Jerry D. Meyer. "Benjamin West's Window Designs for St. George's Chapel, Windsor." *The American Art Journal* 11 (July 1979):53–65.

Oliver Millar. *The Later Georgian Pictures in the Collection of Her Majesty the Queen*. 2 vols. London: Phaidon Press, 1969.

Charles Mitchell. "Benjamin West's *Death of General Wolfe* and the Popular History Piece." *Journal of the Warburg and Courtauld Institutes* 7 (1944):20–33.

Charles Mitchell. "Benjamin West's *Death of Nelson*." *Essays in the History of Art Presented to Rudolf Wittkower*. London: Phaidon Press, 1967, pp. 265–273.

Dennis Montagna. "Benjamin West's *The Death of General Wolfe*: A Nationalist Narrative." *The American Art Journal* 13 (Spring 1981):72–88.

Henry Moses. *The Gallery of Pictures Painted by Benjamin West, Esqr., Historical Painter to His Majesty & President of the Royal Academy: Engraved in Outline by Henry Moses*. London, 1811.

Morton D. Paley. *The Apocalyptic Sublime*. New Haven and London: Yale University Press, 1986.

Nancy L. Pressly. *Revealed Religion: Benjamin West's Commissions for Windsor Castle and Fonthill Abbey* (exhibition catalogue). San Antonio Museum of Art, 1983.

E.P. Richardson. "West's Voyage to Italy, 1760, and William Allen." *The Pennsylvania Magazine of History and Biography* 102 (1978):3–26.

Robert Rosenblum. *Transformations in Late Eighteenth-Century Art*. Princeton: Princeton University Press, 1967.

William Sawitzky. "The American Work of Benjamin West." *The Pennsylvania Magazine of History and Biography* 62 (1938):433–462.

Allen Staley. "The Landing of Agrippina with the Ashes of Germanicus." *Philadelphia Museum of Art Bulletin*, Fall 1965–Winter 1966, pp. 10–19.

Allen Staley. "West's *Death on the Pale Horse*." *Bulletin of the Detroit Institute of Arts* 68 (1980):137–149.

Roy Strong. *Recreating the Past: British History and the Victorian Painter*. New York: Thames and Hudson and The Pierpont Morgan Library, 1978.

Ellis Waterhouse. *Painting in Britain 1530 to 1790*. Harmondsworth, England: The Pelican History of Art, 1953.

Edgar Wind. "The Revolution of History Painting." *Journal of the Warburg and Courtauld Institutes* 2 (1938–1939):116–127.

PHOTOGRAPHY CREDITS

Sources of photographs are cited alphabetically. Photographic material not specifically cited was provided courtesy of the respective owners.

E. Irving Blomstrann, New Britain, Connecticut: page 103.
Michael Bodycomb: page 56.
The British Museum: page 48.
The Brooklyn Museum: page 66.
A.C. Cooper Ltd., London: page 26.
P. Richard Eells: page 32.
Helga Photo Studio, Upper Montclair, New Jersey: page 81.
David J. Henry: page 95.
Paulus Leeser: page 90.
Photo Studios Ltd., London: pages 2, 43.
Nathan Rabin, New York: page 70.
David H. Ramsey, Charlotte: page 74.
Duane Suter, Baltimore: cover and pages 12, 17, 23, 37, 71, 78, 82, 109, 112, 115–117.
Joseph Szaszfai, Branford, Connecticut: pages 42, 86.
Rodney Todd-White & Son, London: page 79.

Printed in an edition of 3,000 copies.

Typography in Bembo and Centaur by Monotype Composition Company, Baltimore.

Color separations by Prolith International, Laurel, Maryland.

Text paper is Warren's Lustro offset dull enamel, 100 pound; cover is 12 pt. Warren's Lusterkote; end papers are Strathmore Grandee Valencia Red, 80 pound text. Text and cover papers are acid-free.

Printing by Schneidereith & Sons, Baltimore.

Design by CASTRO/ARTS, Baltimore.